O9-AIE-684

Teaching Kids about God

*An age-by-age plan for
parents of children
from birth to age twelve*

Tyndale House Publishers, Inc.
CAROL STREAM, ILLINOIS

Visit Tyndale's exciting Web site at www.tyndale.com

TYNDALE and Tyndale's quill logo are registered trademarks of Tyndale House Publishers, Inc.

Teaching Kids about God

A Focus on the Family book published by Tyndale House Publishers, Inc.

Cover photographs copyright © 2003 by David Difuntorum. All rights reserved.

Focus on the Family is a registered trademark of Focus on the Family, Colorado Springs, Colorado.

Library of Congress Cataloging-in-Publications Data

Teaching kids about God : an age by age plan for parents of children from birth to age twelve / general editors, John Trent, Rick Osborne, Kurt Bruner.
     p. cm.
  ISBN-13: 978-0-8423-7679-2 (sc)
  ISBN-10: 0-8423-7679-8 (sc)
  1. Christian education of children.   2. Parenting—Religious aspects—Christianity.   3. Family—Religious aspects—Christianity.   I. Trent, John T.   II. Osborne, Rick.   III. Bruner, Kurt D.
BV1475.3 .T43 2003
248.8[4]5—dc21   2002153986

Printed in the United States of America

10   09   08   07   06
9   8   7   6   5   4

Acknowledgments

This project has been a partnership in the fullest sense of the word, involving Focus on the Family, Lightwave Publishing, Encouraging Words, and Tyndale House Publishers. We wish to thank the following individuals for their help:

--- FOCUS ON THE FAMILY ---

Kurt Bruner
For his passion and vision for this project, his valuable insight, his leadership, and his writing.

John Duckworth
For his invaluable work editing and rewriting.

Jim Mhoon
For managing the project and keeping everyone and everything on track (perhaps the hardest job of all!).

Al Janssen
For leading the Focus editorial team and for his contributions to this work.

Larry Weeden
For reviewing content early on and giving valuable input.

Edie Hutchinson and Jennifer Hurrell
For guiding the packaging and launch of the Guide and Heritage Builders tools.

Lissa Johnson
For writing many of the stories that give this book life.

Ken Janzen and John Perrodin
For review of the completed manuscript.

Jim Weidmann
For important input on the outline and content.

--- ENCOURAGING WORDS ---

John Trent
For his leadership, enthusiasm, and passionate writing.

Marty Kertesz
For her valuable and timely assistance.

--- LIGHTWAVE ---

Rick Osborne
For his passion and vision for the spiritual training of children and for his leadership and writing.

Ken Save
For his whimsical drawings.

Elaine Osborne
For scheduling and organizing this book and the team.

Ed van der Maas (Open Range Editorial)
For his theological and editorial input and for his great work on the charts and forms.

K. Christie Bowler
For her countless hours combing over, compiling, and organizing every word and punctuation mark; and for her great contribution in writing portions of this book.

Andrew Jaster
For his many hours on the computer bringing all these ideas together.

Terry Van Roon
For his wonderful ability to make a large book look inviting, enjoyable, and easy to use.

Kevin Miller
For his assistance in writing and research.

Mikal Marrs and Ed Strauss
For their editorial assistance.

TYNDALE HOUSE

Doug Knox
For sharing the vision.

Jan Long Harris
For editorial support and input.

Thanks to all of you for a job well done!
Focus on the Family

Table of Contents

Introduction

The Single Most Important Task for Christian Parents

For better or worse, you are responsible for much more than you bargained for back when you decided to start a family. With the esteemed title "Mommy" or "Daddy" comes a tremendous responsibility. Now that you have been thrust into the most important role of your life, your everyday choices suddenly have long-term implications for your children. Like it or not, you are faced with the realization that, for good or bad, parents influence the lives of future generations in ways they can't even imagine. No pressure—it's all part of the job!

Throughout the progression from diapers to diplomas, there is one overarching issue that confronts every Christian parent: the spiritual growth of our children. We read in Proverbs 22:6, "Train a child in the way he should go, and when he is old he will not turn from it," and we realize that we're not all that clear on what it means. We have promised ourselves that we won't make the same mistakes our parents made with us, but beyond that we're most likely hard-pressed to come up with a clear, coherent, biblical statement of what is involved in teaching a child to choose the right path.

> Throughout the progression from diapers to diplomas, there is one overarching issue that confronts every Christian parent: the spiritual growth of our children.

At this point you may think, *What about the church? Isn't the spiritual training of our kids the church's responsibility? After all, that's what pastors are trained for, right?*

It's true that pastors across our country are effectively teaching and preaching God's Word and lighting up many lives as a result. But they'd be the first to tell you that the spiritual training of children was never meant to be relegated to a single hour on Sunday morning. Rather, spiritual training was meant to be lived out every day before children by loving parents and grandparents.

PICKING UP THE TORCH

In Deuteronomy 6 we read that communicating our love for God to our children is supposed to happen in the home during the course of everyday life: "Love the LORD your God with all your heart and with all your soul and with all your strength. These commandments that I give you today are to be upon your hearts. Impress them on your children. Talk about them when you sit at home and when you walk along the road, when you lie down and when you get up" (vv. 5-7).

The plain truth is that it is our responsibility as parents to be the primary spiritual trainers of our own children. That task isn't reserved for seminary graduates or those from a long line of faith. It is meant for every person wearing the label "Mommy" or "Daddy."

> Our responsibility as parents is to be the primary spiritual trainers of our own children.

But how am I supposed to be a spiritual trainer for my children? you ask. *I've never been to seminary or taught a Bible class. How do I "train a child in the way he should go" when no one modeled how to do that for me?*

Don't panic! To train up a child to know Jesus, to love Him, and to serve Him doesn't take the knowledge of a professional theologian. It just requires the commitment to start the process and become intentional. Whether you're a new believer or have been a Christian for many years, you may not know all the answers. That's okay. Teaching your children can present a great opportunity to learn more about your faith—right alongside your kids.

You've got the number one advantage: you're there! You're the one on the spot to help your kids through all the challenges that come up at home and at school and in the neighborhood. You're the one who's handy to handle those "teachable moments" when your child has a question about God or faith or Christians.

Teaching spiritual truth to your children—teaching them to know, love, and serve Jesus—can be fun, exciting, and, most of all, life-changing (and one of the lives that will be changing will be your own!). The psalmist prays, "You will fill me with joy in your presence" (Psalm

16:11), and our Lord Himself tells us, "I have come that [you] may have life, and have it to the full" (John 10:10).

Your challenge is to help your children fall in love with Jesus and experience His abundantly full life. So don't wait to become intentional about passing down your faith. Spiritual training isn't going to happen by accident. It will happen because you've decided to begin the process in your own home, to help your children grow up loving the Lord and eventually pass down their faith to their children, your grandchildren.

You *can* shape your children's views of God and give them a solid foundation with Him. Through prayer, patience, and a positive plan designed for your unique family, you can take on the role of spiritual trainer in your home.

NOT JUST HOW, BUT *WHAT*

Knowing how to teach isn't the only thing a parent needs to know. What you teach your children can make all the difference—especially when it comes to spiritual training. That's why you'll find in this book the key truths of the Christian faith you'll want to pass on to your children.

The four sections of this book can help you determine which foundational truths your children are ready to absorb, adjusted for their specific ages. It will also show how far along their own relationships with God can be and will give you a framework for understanding what kind of behavior choices you can expect from them at each stage of their spiritual growth.

As you read through this book, you may wonder how you could ever teach these many truths in a lifetime, let alone during your children's preteen years. You may feel your children's abilities or interests don't fit those described for their age levels. You may believe some topics have been overemphasized—and others left out.

No problem! Rest assured that

- You can cover the topics as you like, in the order that suits you, at your own pace. It's a good idea to read through the chapters covering your children's ages in order to get an overview, but feel free to start by choosing just one or two topics that especially interest you and your children now.

- The truths are meant to be communicated in your own words, reflecting your style and feelings. Your children need to understand and apply them, not memorize them.
- Every child is unique, developing at his or her own speed. Don't worry if your kids don't seem able to grasp a topic that's listed at their age level. Simply wait until they can. The important thing is for them to grow in their relationship with God, not just to learn facts.
- Your outlook, experience, denominational background—all these will influence how you choose to emphasize, de-emphasize, or add to the topics in this section.

As you read, you may discover truths you didn't know. That's great! See this as an opportunity to learn along with your children. Spiritual training isn't just for children; it's for all of us who want to better know and serve the God who loves us.

There's no more wonderful adventure than growing in Christ. If you haven't discovered that in your own spiritual journey, you will as you grow through shaping your child's spiritual experience. Look for the gift of joy in God's presence and the pleasures of living with God forever. Those who seek Him always find Him.

PART 1

—

From Hugs to Hosannas:
What Your 0-4-Year-Old Can Learn about God

CHAPTER 1

- - - - - - - -

The Firm Foundation
of God's Love

The first years of your child's development present a wonderful opportunity for laying a spiritual foundation. Children acquire an astonishing amount of information and skills in these earliest years, and the foundation of what they will learn and experience spiritually in their lives can be well established during this open-door time.

The foundation you want to lay for your children during these first four years of spiritual training is primarily one of love. Most of all, your children need to understand that they are loved, accepted, and wanted—by you and also by a real, caring, and powerful God. These early years are the best time to build into your children the knowledge of God's reality, care, and power.

DEVELOPMENTAL DISTINCTIVES

So how does that helpless, totally dependent newborn turn into a high-powered, skillful four-year-old? With incredible, rapid assimilation of skills and information about the world around him! Think how little resemblance there is between a helpless, incommunicative baby and a talkative, eager preschooler. These are some wonderful years for learning.

PHYSICAL AND MENTAL DEVELOPMENT

Newborns aren't idle layabouts. They are hard at work learning about their bodies and this strange place they're in. And they are working on a number of key tasks: forming an attachment bond (first with Mom), learning they are accepted, developing autonomy or independence and a sense of initiation—the ability to discover things on their own.

> Most of all, your children need to understand that they are loved, accepted, and wanted—by you and also by a real, caring, and powerful God.

By age two they have a brain that is 75 percent of its adult size. They walk, run, climb, pedal a tricycle, use objects to represent other objects, play alone while interacting little with others, develop a recognizable personality, begin to talk, and are mental sponges.

By three they have a vocabulary of 500 to 1,000 words, form sentences of five and more words, add about 50 words a month to their vocabulary, and are still mental sponges.

At age four they skip awkwardly; have greater strength, endurance, and coordination; draw shapes and stick figures; paint pictures; build with blocks; play interactively; have laid the basic foundations of life; are in a growth spurt so need lots of exercise; discover friends; feed themselves; almost completely dress themselves; go to the bathroom alone; express emotions that change from minute to minute; can think of God in a personal way; and can trust Him with a simple faith.

SPIRITUAL DEVELOPMENT

One way to think about spiritual growth is to imagine that each child has an empty photo album that needs pictures. Although God created your children as unique individuals, from the first moment you hold them you are adding to their album and forming their picture of the world. When you protect them and love them by caring for their basic needs, they learn that they are loved and the world is a safe place. They need to know this is also true spiritually, so you need to demonstrate, with actions and words, that God is like you: He also cares for them, keeps them safe, and makes sure their needs are met. When they hear and see this repeatedly, they begin to build a worldview with a Christian foundation that sets them up for life.

Sadly, if this foundation isn't actively established at this stage, the child will build up some other idea of foundation, such as, "I have to take care of myself."

In these early years your children are dependent on you to feed and nourish them spiritually. Begin to pray for your child immediately—beginning when you are pregnant if possible. Pray short, simple prayers out loud over your baby and persistently affirm God's love and care. When you consistently pray for your children, they learn what prayer is and that God is interested in them. You can begin this even before your children know what talking is. Simply thank God for them out loud, pray that He gives them a good sleep, and thank Him for putting them in your life. In doing this you are giving them the basics of the Christian faith: God is real, He made them and loves them, He takes care of them, and prayer is talking to God.

You as parents are giving your children their first snapshots of life. It's probably a collage-quilt of impressions—love, comfort, security, smiles and frowns, happiness, care—all pieced together within a bright border that says, "Mommy, Daddy, and God love me. I'm special." What a way to start off their life's photo album!

KEY WAYS TO PREPARE THEIR HEARTS

Between birth and kindergarten, children are ultimately receptive. You are doing all the work of preparing them for a lifelong relationship with God by loving, nurturing, reassuring, and caring for them. Children are all very different, but they are similar in their needs, what they can understand, how they develop, and what approaches work best.

Be consistent. An important element of love and nurture, both physical and spiritual, is consistency. Make a habit of telling your children of your love and God's. Consistency is key because it's impossible to tell when any child starts to understand what you're doing. But if you're constantly modeling a positive attitude toward God and a loving relationship with Him, you will be doing that when your child starts to notice. And you will also be modeling who God is: faithful and continuously present.

Model God's love as you show your love. In this love and nurture stage, it's impossible to overemphasize the importance of modeling.

Growth is a continuum. It begins with you modeling who God is and what a relationship with Him is like as you demonstrate your love and God's love. You do this as you care for your children, talk with them, and show them what love is. They observe and take it in.

> These early years are the best time to build into your children the knowledge of God's reality, care, and power.

As they start understanding language, you verbally communicate that you love them and God loves them. Then you gently move your children to where they begin to interact with God themselves. Even before they can comprehend what you're saying, you can continually explain the basic truths to them (such as what prayer is). Your intentional modeling raises questions for them that you can answer in a nurturing, loving environment.

Finally, your children will try to imitate you. It's a natural cycle of growth especially obvious in this stage.

Connect with your children where they are, and connect over what they're interested in. This growth continuum happens in all areas. They learn most when your teaching connects with their current thoughts and interests. For example, when you pray over your children, explain what you're doing, and encourage questions. Then you let them join you. This might be as simple as asking them what they want to pray about and then praying their prayers for them, such as, "Dear God, thank You for loving me. Help me go potty in the potty and sleep well." This prayer connects with them because it deals with their concerns and is short and simple enough for them to grasp. Of course, their prayers may be longer and cover more ground than this one, but it's a good idea not to stretch prayer time and content past their limited attention span. Stay at your child's "heart level." Gradually, as you explain and answer questions, your children will want to pray their own prayers.

Teach obedience. At this stage, it's also important to establish the principle of obedience to parents, in the context of love and nurture. One of the ways God loves and cares for His children is by teaching them and giving them guidelines. You teach your children to be obedient to God because you know He loves them and is trustworthy. They should also obey you because, like God, you love them and want the best for them. Children live so much out of their emotions and are so intent on exploring their world, learning the limits, and becoming independent that obedience is hard for them at first. They will need help. Gently walk them through the right response again and again—and again.

Keep learning exciting. Spark and enliven your children's interest in God and spiritual ideas by employing different media such as simple Bible videos or music tapes. Spice things up by adding actions, playing games, or giving them a snack during their video. Try singing together in the car, or playing a game with their hands and feet reminding them that God made our bodies. As you walk them in the stroller, talk about all the things you see and communicate God's great artistry and creativity. Use variety to increase their enjoyment and keep their interest high. Use Bible stories that are suited to their level. Talk with them about the pictures and what they mean. Relate what you're talking about to their lives.

Make their church experience appealing. Do what you can to get clothes, offering, and breakfast ready on Saturday night to limit the rush and stress of Sunday morning. Work with your church to ensure that the nursery and early-childhood classrooms are attractive—bright and exciting. Make sure your children aren't simply being baby-sat but are learning simple songs and Bible stories. Volunteer to help in the nursery. Work to make church an enjoyable experience for your kids.

COMMON REFLECTIONS OF FAITH AT THIS AGE

Nothing beats the thrill of observing your children's faith in development. Happily, you will be able to see reflections of their spiritual development.

As your children grow, they'll move toward the next stage, where they will become more actively involved in their own faith and learning. On the way there, they will enjoy the various things you're doing together with them and God, such as praying, reading Bible storybooks, and singing songs, and they will begin to want to "do it myself" rather than having you do it all for them. They will start to grasp some of the basics about God and the Christian faith: They'll understand certain things about how God wants them to be and behave, know that God loves them and made them (and everything else) on purpose, and know that they can talk to God.

MEMORY MARKERS

Celebrate your children's spiritual development by building intentional remembrances of the growth that you see in faith and relationship with God. One excellent way to do this is to establish some "memory markers."

In the Old Testament, Joshua's first day on the job included a faith-stretching task. Taking over from Moses, he was to lead the people across the Jordan River at flood stage. Years earlier, God had enabled Moses to part the Red Sea so Israel could escape slavery. Now God told Joshua and the priests that He would part the waters again. Not only did almighty God provide a way of escape from Egypt, He parted the waters for the Israelites' entrance into the land that He'd promised to Abraham so long ago.

Once Joshua and the priests had everyone safely across, God commanded His new leader to set up a "Memory Marker." Twelve stones from the middle of the riverbed were to be made into a special marker to commemorate what God had done. But the stones weren't just to celebrate that day—and they weren't just for Joshua and the people who crossed the river.

[Joshua] said to the Israelites, "In the future when your descendants ask their fathers, 'What do these stones mean?' tell them, 'Israel crossed the Jordan on dry ground.' For the LORD your God dried up the Jordan before you until you had crossed over. The LORD your God did to the Jordan just what he had done to the Red Sea when he dried it up before us until we had crossed over. He did this so that all the peoples of the earth might know that the hand of the LORD is powerful and so that you might always fear the LORD your God." (Joshua 4:21-24)

The "Memory Marker" Joshua was commanded to put up was a picture for the children of Israel. That pile of rocks became a testimony to what God had done and an opportunity for parents and children to focus on God's greatness and love. It was a snapshot of God's faithfulness that they could look at and talk about.

You can create similar "markers" or "snapshots" for the members of your family.

DEDICATION

One common but powerful Memory Marker is a formal dedication. Just as Hannah, the mother of Samuel, dedicated her son to the Lord (1 Samuel 1) and Mary presented Jesus to God (Luke 2:21-38), so you can commit your children to God and commit yourself to raising them with His help. Children will, of course, decide for themselves eventually, but in dedicating them to God, you also commit yourself to doing everything you can throughout their lives to teach and train them to follow God, lead Christ-centered lives, and develop their own personal relationship with Him. By dedicating them to God, you are dedicating yourself to taking up the calling God has given you and making your own commitment to love and nurture them. By giving your children to God, you are acknowledging His partnership in the parenting process and asking for His help and wisdom.

Usually children are dedicated when they are infants or toddlers—

too early for them to remember it on their own. But with photographs or video and the memories of family members who joined in the dedication, your children will have lots of help remembering.

LIFELONG PROMISE

If your child is being dedicated, consider choosing a "life verse" for him or her. Here are a few ideas:

- Psalm 19:14 ("May the words of my mouth and the meditation of my heart be pleasing in your sight, O LORD, my Rock and my Redeemer.")

- Psalm 139:23-24 ("Search me, O God, and know my heart; test me and know my anxious thoughts. See if there is any offensive way in me, and lead me in the way everlasting.")

- Proverbs 3:5-6 ("Trust in the LORD with all your heart and lean not on your own understanding; in all your ways acknowledge him, and he will make your paths straight.")

- Jeremiah 29:11 (" 'For I know the plans I have for you,' declares the LORD, 'plans to prosper you and not to harm you, plans to give you hope and a future.' ")

- Ephesians 3:17-19 ("I pray that you, being rooted and established in love, may have power, together with all the saints, to grasp how wide and long and high and deep is the love of Christ, and to know this love that surpasses knowledge—that you may be filled to the measure of all the fullness of God.")

Many churches incorporate the dedication of babies into their worship service, with a pastor or elder praying for the baby, for the parents, and for the whole congregation who will share in the Christian education of the baby.

Consider choosing a "life verse" for each of your children to read at their dedications—something that you can note in their memory books, on their dedication certificates, or in their first Bible storybooks. Choose Bible verses that embody your hopes and prayers for them.

When your children are old enough, tell them about the special verses you chose for them, show them the snapshots or video of their dedication services, and explain how you promised to train them in God's ways.

THINGS ABOUT GOD THEY'RE READY TO LEARN

This chart points the way to the next three chapters, which will explain what your infant-to-preschool children are ready to learn.

- The "Knowing" columns contain truths about their faith, God, and what He has done;
- the "Loving" column is about developing their relationship with God;
- and the "Living" columns are about living out in their person and actions who God wants them to be.

In each of these three areas, topics and concepts are listed that your children can grasp. Amazed? Don't be surprised! Your little sponges can absorb all of these spiritual truths, as you'll see in the chapters ahead.

Ages 0–4

KNOWING		LOVING	LIVING	
A. Who God Is	B. What God Has Done	C. You Can Have a Relationship with God	D. You Can Be All God Wants You to Be	E. You Can Do All God Wants You to Do
1. God exists. 2. God loves you. 3. Jesus loves you. 4. God wants to take care of you.	5. God created everything. 6. God created you. 7. God gave us the Bible. 8. God's Son, Jesus, died for your sins so you can be with God.	9. Prayer is talking to God in Jesus' name. 10. You need to talk to God regularly. 11. You need to regularly listen to stories about God and Jesus from the Bible.	12. God wants you to be good, kind, and loving, just like Him and Jesus. 13. God wants you to see and think good things.	14. God wants you to go to church. 15. God wants you to obey your parents. 16. God wants you to learn to share your things with others.

CHAPTER 2

- - - - - - - - -

Knowing

What Preschoolers Can Know about God and Their Faith

What your preschooler can know has two parts. Your preschooler can know who God is, and she can know what He has done. God's character and personality is a great place for believers of any age to begin to grow in their faith, so it is an incredible blessing for a child to absorb this information in the years between ages zero and four.

LEARNING WHO GOD IS

What do infants and toddlers need most? To be loved, accepted, and safe. Affirming that God loves and cares for them can begin the day your children are born. As you hold them, love them, feed them, and keep them warm, you establish that their world is good and safe. In time, as you tell them that God loves them and looks after them, they make the connection between your loving behaviors and God's active love for them.

GOD EXISTS.

The primary way that your little ones will learn that God is real and He is really there is from your behavior. As you constantly acknowledge

God's reality and presence, your child will readily accept what you believe so thoroughly. Your constant communication with God—at mealtimes, at bedtimes, at times of stress or need—are everyday reminders that God is there, listening. Your constant communication about God—explaining where trees and squirrels and the oceans came from and who is in control of the wind and the rain—firmly establishes your child's understanding that God is real.

Bedtime is ideal for thinking about God's presence. Try talking aloud to God as you rock your baby or give your toddler a back rub. At first your children won't know who God is because they can't see Him. But as you affirm His existence and love with verbal, visible, and emotional demonstrations, they'll take His existence for granted.

> The primary way that your little ones will learn that God is real and He is really there is from your behavior.

When your child is old enough, you can walk him through the Scriptures that depend so completely on God's sovereign reality. The very first words of Scripture are "In the beginning God" (Genesis 1:1). Tell your child that God's reality is so evident in His creation that God expects people to know Him: "For since the creation of the world God's invisible qualities—his eternal power and divine nature—have been clearly seen, being understood from what has been made, so that men are without excuse" (Romans 1:20).

GOD LOVES YOU; JESUS LOVES YOU.

How can you teach your children that God loves them? With hugs, smiles, and telling them you love them! Thus they learn what *love* means. As you add that God loves them, they'll know what that means too. The primary avenue for teaching God's love to your toddler is by your own loving actions. Tell your children you love them, and show it in your words and actions. Tell them, then, where love comes from—the Creator: "We love because he first loved us" (1 John 4:19). Sing "God Is So Good" and other songs that affirm God's love.

Preschoolers may have difficulty separating the idea of Jesus' love from that of God's love—and that's just fine because, of course, Jesus is God. But go ahead and sing "Jesus Loves Me, This I Know" and "Jesus Loves the Little Children" with your children. And tell them that Jesus showed us God's love: "For God so loved the world that he gave his one and only Son" (John 3:16).

GOD WANTS TO TAKE CARE OF YOU.

The way Jesus taught His followers about God's desire to care and provide for them was by pointing out the provisions of nature: "Look at the birds of the air; they do not sow or reap or store away in barns, and yet your heavenly Father feeds them. Are you not much more valuable than they? . . . See how the lilies of the field grow. They do not labor or spin. Yet I tell you that not even Solomon in all his splendor was dressed like one of these. If that is how God clothes the grass of the field, which is here today and tomorrow is thrown into the fire, will he not much more clothe you, O you of little faith?" (Matthew 6:26, 28-30). You can also point out God's sovereign care and control over nature.

When your children feel sick, affirm God's care and provision by comforting them, saying you care and that you want them to feel better. They'll see what "caring about them" means. When you add that God cares and wants them to feel better, they'll understand.

If you're feeling uncertain about God's love and care yourself—perhaps due to money problems, illness, or other tough times—give yourself time to deal with your doubts. Try reading in the Gospels (Matthew, Mark, Luke, and John) to discover through the example of Jesus that God is loving, compassionate, kind, welcoming, forgiving, generous, healing, and providing. He desires to be all these things in your family's life. You may also want to work through your uncertainties with your pastor or a Christian counselor. Ask God to help you trust Him so that you can aid your children in doing the same.

LEARNING WHAT GOD HAS DONE

So much of what we know about God stems from what we have seen Him do! Just as your children are convinced that you are trustworthy and consistent—since you've proved it by your actions—your children will become assured of God's power and creativity and generosity by seeing how He has acted. So introduce your toddler and preschool children to what God has done.

GOD CREATED EVERYTHING. GOD CREATED YOU.

We all need to know that we're wanted and unique. So even before your children understand, tell them that God made them special. This shows His care for them and strengthens their sense of personal value. Let them know that God not only made them but that He made them purposefully and lovingly.

Tell them that God made everything else, too. This fact is your children's first glimpse of God's power and bigness.

A three-year-old could even learn the very first verse of Scripture: "In the beginning God created the heavens and the earth" (Genesis 1:1),

and most of your children's Bible storybooks will include the account of God's creation of the world and of people (Genesis 1:1-31).

Review the concepts found in Psalm 139, especially verses 13 through 16. Teach your children the truth of verse 13: "For you created my inmost being; you knit me together in my mother's womb."

When you pray for and over your children, thank God for making them so special and for giving them to you and your family. Be as specific as you can. For example, at the end of a day in which your toddler built an especially tall tower of blocks, thank God for giving him or her a steady hand and a creative mind.

Do your children like to see how tall they are, perhaps standing next to you or a height chart, or just looking in the mirror? Use these times to point out specific things about your children that God designed, such as eyes and mouth, ability to laugh and have fun, nose shape, and hair color.

"God made everything" can be a tough concept for children at the younger end of this age group to grasp, since "everything" is so vast. So be concrete, pointing out individual items He made—a tree, flowers, mountains, other people, a pet. Choose things your child likes or is curious about.

GOD GAVE US THE BIBLE.

Why do your children need to know early on that the Bible is God's book? Because it will be so basic to their relationship with God. It's a one-of-a-kind book that only God could have written, and He wrote it for His much-loved people, including you and your family!

Children also need to know that God's book is true; it's not simply a storybook like others they look at or have read to them. Except for certain stories, such as parables, the events in the Bible really happened—and the people in it were real. As you prepare to communicate this truth about God's Word to your children, review it yourself, investigating verses such as Psalm 33:4, Psalm 119:160, Joshua 1:8, and 1 Thessalonians 2:13. Remember where the words of the Scriptures come from: "All Scripture is God-breathed" (2 Timothy 3:16).

> Children need to know that God's book is true; it's not simply a storybook like others they look at.

As your children start with the simplest board books, give them simple Bible storybooks, too. Let them see your "grown-up" Bible and those of older siblings, explaining what these are and how you enjoy them. Help your toddler look forward to getting older and owning a Bible that has more of God's story in it.

When possible, choose Bible storybooks that take your children from the beginning (creation and Adam and Eve) to the end (Jesus' res-

urrection, the growth of the church, and Jesus' return) and books that introduce the Bible's main characters. This helps young-sters to see that God's Word is more than a collection of unrelated events and people.

Help your children understand the idea of "true" stories by saying something like, "I'm your Mommy (or Daddy). You're my child, and you live in Mommy's (and/or Daddy's) house. That's a true story." Recount a recent incident involving the children and explain that this, too, is a true story. This prepares chil-dren to understand what you mean when you say that the Bible and the stories in it are true.

GOD'S SON, JESUS, DIED FOR YOUR SINS SO YOU CAN BE WITH GOD.

When your children are three and four, they will easily grasp the basic "good news" story. You might express it this way: "Everyone, even you, does some wrong things. These wrong things are sin and make God sad. But God loves us so much that He sent His Son, Jesus. Jesus died for us so that we could be forgiven and could be God's children. Just as you need to tell me you're sorry when you've done something wrong, you need to tell God you're sorry for doing wrong things and ask Him to for-give you. He will. From then on, you are God's child. And if you do any-thing wrong after that, you can ask God to forgive you and help you do better—and He will."

Your preschooler is still too young to learn that foundational verse about salvation, John 3:16 ("For God so loved the world that he gave his one and only Son, that whoever believes in him shall not perish but have eternal life"), but you could teach your child the two ideas found in 1 John 4:10: "God loved us" and "God sent Jesus to take away our sins" (paraphrased).

No doubt you will have spent such a large amount of training time in these years that your child will already be aware of what sins are—behaviors that don't please God. Do you use time-outs, spankings, or lost privileges to discipline your child? Try mentioning these as you explain the concept of sin and how Jesus paid the price for ours. Children will understand how wrong acts displease God because they know how you respond when they disobey. Explain that wrong actions put a wide space between your children and God—one that they can't cross alone. Talk about every person's need for God, and how we can never be clean enough for God without His help ("For all have sinned and fall short of the glory of God" and "For the wages of sin is death, but the gift of God is eternal life in Christ Jesus our Lord"—Romans 3:23; 6:23). That's why Jesus came—to make a way for them to cross back to God and be forgiven. If your children have already accepted Jesus, emphasize that they can go to God anytime, about anything, and ask Him to forgive them when they've done something wrong.

Younger children may be baffled by the idea that Jesus "died on the cross," especially if they don't understand what death is. If you sense that a discussion of death would scare, rather than inform, your preschooler, concentrate on talking about the love and actions of Jesus, especially the fact that He came to rescue us. When your child is ready to understand what it meant for Jesus to give His life, explain that part of the salvation story.

CHAPTER 3

-- -- -- -- -- -- -- --

Loving

Preschoolers Can Have a Relationship with God

Many people wonder how early a child actually can understand salvation and trust Christ for it, but most adult believers who were saved as young children credit these earliest years as a true beginning of their personal relationship with God. It is never too early for God's created people to do the very thing he created them for: have a deep friendship with Him. Help your child grow in relationship with God in the same way you're growing in relationship with Him—through prayer and knowing God's Word. Here are a few more truths your toddler/preschooler can absorb.

DEVELOPING A FRIENDSHIP WITH GOD

PRAYER IS TALKING TO GOD IN JESUS' NAME; YOU NEED TO TALK TO GOD REGULARLY.

How do young children learn about relationships? By watching and interacting with you! Explain that just as the closeness between you and your children grows as you spend time talking, so closeness to God grows through prayer—and prayer is simply talking to God. You'll want to

mention a few specifics about prayer; for instance, it often helps to close your eyes when you do it, to help you concentrate. And prayers often include the words "in Jesus' name" because Jesus is the One whose sacrifice made it possible for us to be close to God.

Let children know that God hears them and wants to help them, just as you hear and want to help. But God is much bigger than you are, and He knows best how to take care of them. They can talk to Him about anything; God loves to hear from them, just as you do. And since being close to God is so important, talking with Him needs to go on the list of things we do every day.

We've already mentioned simple ways to incorporate prayer starting from your child's first days, but you may want to make a point of showing your three- or four-year-old the actual words in Scripture that say "Pray continually" (1 Thessalonians 5:17). While your little one learns that verse, you can meditate on this one: "Do not be anxious about anything, but in everything, by prayer and petition, with thanksgiving, present your requests to God. And the peace of God, which transcends all understanding, will guard your hearts and your minds in Christ Jesus" (Philippians 4:6-7).

> Since being close to God is so important, talking with Him needs to go on the list of things we do every day.

Before your children have learned to speak, let them hear you pray as often as you can. In addition to mealtimes and bedtimes, try praying at "odd" times—perhaps carrying them from the car to their room as they're falling asleep, or when you encounter a beautiful cloud formation during a walk. In the car as you're driving, you might say, "Oh, thank you, God, for the rain we need so much," or "Thank you, Lord, for the sunshine!" As you establish the habit of prayer, your children will be more likely to pick it up.

As much as possible, let praying be easy and enjoyable—even fun! While uncontrollable giggles can spoil a prayer time, feel free to pray about funny things that happened during the day—for example, thanking God that you got to share a "Knock, Knock" joke or see the dog chasing its tail. To fit attention spans at this age, try to keep your prayers short and to the point.

Be yourself! Prayer doesn't have to be formal or use certain words. When you pray with your children, favor words and language that are part of their normal, everyday speech—and yours. Requiring formal, unfamiliar language implies that God is "foreign" and unknowable and that children must put on an act in His presence. Allow your prayers to reflect your feelings, too; if you're excited, for instance, let it show!

At the younger end of this stage, it's likely that you'll say the prayers and your children will listen. Let them know that these are their prayers and that you are praying in order to show them how to do it. Ask children what they'd like you to pray about. As children progress through this stage, move them toward praying with you. Near the end of this stage, help them begin to pray their own prayers.

Pray about anything and everything, especially things that already interest your children. For example, if a child is learning to clean up his toys, pray, "Dear God, help Jimmy to be a big boy and put his toys away." This leads children to realize that God cares about the things that are important to them.

From time to time, take a break from prayer itself to remind children why you're praying—and to whom. Remind them that God is really there, listening, and that they don't have to work hard to get their prayers through to Him. He's ready and willing to answer.

*YOU NEED TO REGULARLY LISTEN TO STORIES ABOUT GOD
AND JESUS FROM THE BIBLE.*

Have you learned to love God's Word? Your own love for Scripture will grow as you shape your child's interest in and desire for the Bible. A yearning for God's truths is reflected throughout Psalm 119. Verses 130-31 say, "The unfolding of your words gives light; it gives understanding to the simple. I open my mouth and pant, longing for your commands." Let your children catch that kind of enthusiasm from you!

> Have you learned to love God's Word? Your own love for Scripture will grow as you shape your child's interest in and desire for the Bible.

Even at this age, children can spend time each day focused on God. In the New Testament letters of Paul to Timothy, Paul commends Timothy's mother and grandmother for teaching him God's Word from early childhood: "From infancy you have known the holy Scriptures, which are able to make you wise for salvation through faith in Christ Jesus" (2 Timothy 3:15). As parents, you can be like those godly women by consistently reading to your children from a Bible storybook—or by telling them Bible stories yourself! When you do, remind them why you are doing it: so they can learn more about God and get to know Him. Explain that God's Book tells them what He's like, how He acts, and how He wants them to act.

If you can tell Bible stories on your own, make the experience fun! Let your children add sound effects (stomping feet for thunder, slapping knees for rain, etc.). Include as much drama and expression in your voice as you can. Older children in this stage may also be able to tell the stories back to you!

To remind your children that a Bible or Bible storybook is different from other books, approach it differently. Before you open it, try asking God to help you and your children understand what you read. This will also serve as a good model later as they begin to read the Bible on their own.

If the Bible storybook you're using provides a lesson, deal with it briefly and try to relate it to the day's events. It's not necessary to pull a "lesson" out of each story, however. Be open to children's questions, allowing time for and encouraging discussion.

CHAPTER 4

- - - - - - - - - -

Living

How Preschoolers Can Live Out Their Faith

Young children live out their faith in the same way we grown-ups do—by *being* Christ-followers and *doing* what pleases God. Toddlers and preschoolers are not too young to choose willfully to direct their heart attitudes and their behavior choices in the direction of godliness, as opposed to pleasing themselves. All grown-ups know that this choosing God's way over our own way is a lifelong discipline of the Christian life, so it's exciting to see little ones taking early steps in paths of righteousness.

BEING ALL GOD WANTS YOU TO BE

GOD WANTS YOU TO BE GOOD, KIND, AND LOVING, JUST LIKE HIM AND JESUS.

Your children may learn quickly that there's a right way of behaving. But do they know there's a right way of being? Correct behavior comes out of correct being. The perfect model for being and behavior is God Himself—as Jesus, His Son, has shown us. Jesus tells us, "Love each other as

I have loved you" (John 15:12). He holds Himself up as the primary guide and example for our behavior.

When your children do something wrong, focus on saying and demonstrating what they should have done, not just on what they did wrong. Say something like "Next time we can do it God's way." Be brief with this process, quickly moving on to hugs and fun things that reinforce your expectation that they will want to follow the example of Jesus.

For younger children, you'll need to show what it means to be kind, good, and loving. For example, if two-year-old Marie hits brother Ken on the head, kneel down at Marie's level and give her a brief lesson on the topic of touch. Say something like "When you touch people, you need to be kind and gentle, like Jesus. If you want to touch Ken, this is how you should do it." Take her hand and help her pat Ken's arm. Explain that this kind of touch makes a person feel happy and loved.

When talking with your children about being kind and loving, do it in a kind, loving way. It's easy to be harsh when a child has just done wrong, but that doesn't affirm goodness. If necessary, give yourself a few minutes to calm down before speaking. When you do, try to phrase your guidance as positively as you can. For example, affirm that kindness and goodness are part of your family identity: "Because we love Jesus, this is how we act in our family."

GOD WANTS YOU TO SEE AND THINK GOOD THINGS.

Children this age often can't separate what's going on inside (thoughts and feelings) from what comes out (actions). As they progress through the stage, though, you can begin to help them realize that seeing and thinking good, kind, loving things will help them to be good, kind, and loving. This concept derives directly from Scripture, which points to the heart as being the source of our behavior choices: "The good man brings good things out of the good stored up in his heart, and the evil man brings evil things out of the evil stored up in his heart. For out of the overflow of his heart his mouth speaks" (Luke 6:45).

When listening to music or watching TV with your children, pause occasionally to ask how they're feeling. Use their answers as a spring-board to talk about the way we're shaped by what we see and hear. If they're listening to a sad song and feel sad, point out the connection. Do the same if they're upbeat while watching a happy show. Explain that God wants them to see and hear good things because He loves them and wants the best for them.

What can you do when your children copy the actions of others who fight or speak rudely? In addition to dealing with the disobedience itself, use the incident as a chance to explain how what we see and hear can convince us to do the wrong things. Conversely, cheer your children on when they imitate positive behavior; point out that God wants us to watch and listen to such good examples.

DOING ALL GOD WANTS YOU TO DO

GOD WANTS YOU TO GO TO CHURCH.

Church is God's idea, and for good reason! It's meant to be part of every Christian's learning and support system. To show your children that church is vital, involve them in it at the earliest possible age. Take them to the nursery or Sunday school; make sure they're comfortable and se-cure. If your children have trouble staying when you leave, remain and help if you can for the first time or two. Help them enjoy being there so that they'll gain a positive view of church.

As soon as your children can under-stand, tell them why you go to church: to learn about God, to celebrate His greatness, and to be with others who love Him.

Don't have a church? Find one! Your whole family can benefit from the support and the challenge to grow in your faith. Try to find one close enough that your children can participate in activities as they grow. Check out the Sunday school and other children's programs. Look for an enjoyable, exciting environment with an emphasis on helping children learn about God and the Bible.

Get involved in what your children are doing at church. Sit in on some of their classes, helping out if you can. Watch to see that by the time your children are one to two years old, they're learning basic lessons about Jesus through songs, stories, and fun at church. Encourage them to participate in crafts, games, and action songs, and to answer questions when they're able. Try to bring them together with church friends for playtimes, sending the message that it's important and fun to spend time with Christian friends.

> To show your children that church is vital, involve them in it at the earliest possible age.

Whether your church meets on Sunday morning or at another time, try to make that part of the week special. Create fond memories for children to associate with church time—a favorite breakfast, a simple quiz in

- -

LOOKING FOR A CHURCH?

If you're trying to find a church to get involved in as a family, here are some things to consider:

- Ask Christian friends or coworkers—particularly those with children—where they go to church and what they consider to be their church's strengths.

- Look in the yellow pages, then call some of the churches and ask about their children's programs. Many churches provide Awana or other club programs during the week for preschool and school-age children.

- Check the religion section of your local newspaper. Many papers highlight special church events, so you may get a feel for which churches in your area are active and growing.

- When you visit a church, tour the building, especially the children's area. Observe some Sunday school classes or a Children's Church time. How large are the Sunday school classes? Are the teachers pleasant but in control of the class? Are the children enjoying themselves and learning about the Bible? Are there other children close to your children's ages?

- -

the car, a picnic. Plan ahead so you can avoid rushing. Talk with enthusiasm about what you'll be doing at church, and afterward discuss positively what you learned.

Make church a family priority that doesn't get bumped by leisure activities or catching up on sleep! The book of Hebrews encourages believers: "Let us not give up meeting together, as some are in the habit of doing, but let us encourage one another—and all the more as you see the Day approaching" (10:25).

GOD WANTS YOU TO OBEY YOUR PARENTS.

One of the Ten Commandments is to honor mothers and fathers—and honor includes obedience. Those who honor parents are promised long lives: "Children, obey your parents in the Lord, for this is right. 'Honor your father and mother'—which is the first commandment with a promise—'that it may go well with you and that you may enjoy long life on the earth' " (Ephesians 6:1-3; see also Exodus 20:12).

Children need to know that obedience is not optional. In fact, learning to obey you is a key to learning to obey God. At this stage, obeying you is what pleases God: "Children, obey your parents in everything, for this pleases the Lord" (Colossians 3:20).

Show your children how obedience looks. When you're driving, point out the speed-limit sign and how you're obeying the law. When you bring your child to the workplace, explain that you're doing what God wants when you provide for your family. Explain that *you* need to obey too. You obey God, your boss at work, and the government, because obeying is part of God's plan.

As children grow older, they need to trust that when you tell them to do something, you have a good reason for it. When they're able to understand, tell them why they have to do something—not "because I said so," but because it will keep them healthy, give them a skill they'll need, and so on.

Say yes to your children whenever you can. Only say no when you have to—when the issue has to do with safety or growing their character, for example. This reflects God's heart. Ask them to do things that are reasonable and for their good, and be prepared to give them the reasons when they're old enough to understand. This, too, reflects God: Everything He tells us to do is reasonable and for our good. This approach to obedience helps children realize as they grow older that God isn't arbitrary or a killjoy. From your example they will begin to see that God's way is the best way.

> Children need to know that obedience is not optional. In fact, learning to obey you is a key to learning to obey God.

GOD WANTS YOU TO LEARN TO SHARE YOUR THINGS WITH OTHERS.
Brianna, like other toddlers, is just learning that her doll doesn't cease to exist when she can't see it. Before she can feel comfortable sharing her doll, she needs to know it's still there, even when it's being used by someone else.

She also needs to understand that the doll still belongs to her, and that she'll get it back later. A sense of ownership must precede sharing. So for younger children, emphasize two truths: God lets us have nice things, and He wants us to share them with others.

During much of this stage, children tend to play alone or side by side—not interacting together. For them, to share means simply letting another person use their things for a time. Help them know that this makes the other person happy and that they will get the things back. Begin to instill in them the fact that God will take care of their needs; they can trust Him with their belongings and share them.

Sharing and generosity are distinctives of God's people displayed

Ages 0–4

KNOWING		LOVING	LIVING	
A. Who God Is	B. What God Has Done	C. You Can Have a Relationship with God	D. You Can Be All God Wants You to Be	E. You Can Do All God Wants You to Do
1. God exists. 2. God loves you. 3. Jesus loves you. 4. God wants to take care of you.	5. God created everything. 6. God created you. 7. God gave us the Bible. 8. God's Son, Jesus, died for your sins so you can be with God.	9. Prayer is talking to God in Jesus' name. 10. You need to talk to God regularly. 11. You need to regularly listen to stories about God and Jesus from the Bible.	12. God wants you to be good, kind, and loving, just like Him and Jesus. 13. God wants you to see and think good things.	14. God wants you to go to church. 15. God wants you to obey your parents. 16. God wants you to learn to share your things with others.

throughout Scripture. In the Old Testament, sharing and generosity are built right into the thousands of commands God gave the Israelites about living as a community and caring for the needy. Jesus modeled and taught a high level of self-sacrifice. John the Baptist taught, "The man with two tunics should share with him who has none, and the one who has food should do the same" (Luke 3:11). Paul encouraged believers toward wealth, not in material things, but in righteous works: "Command them to do good, to be rich in good deeds, and to be generous and willing to share" (1 Timothy 6:18).

Rather than forcing your children to share a new toy, give them time to enjoy it first. Once they've played with it, sharing will be easier.

Try trading and taking turns. It's a good way to introduce sharing. If Christopher and Jonathan are playing with their own spaceships, have them trade for a minute or so. As they learn that the ships don't disappear when out of their hands and that their belongings will be returned, you can increase the trading time. Or sit with your children and play together, taking brief turns with several toys.

Help children to see the difference between ownership and selfishness. When four-year-old Tanisha refuses to let younger brother Bobby use one of her many crayons, explain why Bobby's request is reasonable. Point out that we need to be in charge of our things without being selfish—just as God has been unselfish with us. In time your children will be able to understand that ultimately God owns everything; just as He shares His possessions with us, He wants us to share with others. This also helps your children start to learn that relationship is more important than things.

WONDER KIDS

Your accomplished learner will absorb so much in the years between birth and kindergarten! Photocopy the chart on page 31 and hang it on your fridge as a constant reminder to yourself of what you want to instill in your child during these crucial training years and what knowledge and behaviors your child can be responsible for.

PART 2

—

From Friendships to Faith:
What Your 5-6-Year-Old Can Learn about God

CHAPTER 5

An Era of Growing Relationships

Your key task during this stage is to help your children have a growing relationship with God and others. Thus far you have been doing everything for your children, but now they're ready for the next step where you take them to God and actively train and teach them to do their part in the task of learning, doing, and growing. It's time to help them become committed to God and develop their own relationship with Him.

When you make God a natural, consistent part of your lives, developing a relationship with Him will come easily for your children as they, too, fall into the practice of including Him. The key is to ensure that God has a significant place in their lives. You need to make sure that they understand how important healthy relationships (with God and others) are, and that they know what those healthy relationships look like and how to build them.

DEVELOPMENTAL DISTINCTIVES

Five- and six-year-old children are becoming social creatures, and although their physical growth is slowing down, they are still developing a vast number of skills and abilities.

PHYSICAL AND MENTAL DEVELOPMENT

At age five, children have generally at least doubled their birth length, weigh from 35 to 50 pounds, feed themselves using silverware, and dress and undress themselves. They're active and agile, print their names, and have a vocabulary of about 2,000 words, although they understand more. Most are friendly and enjoy playing with others. Adult approval and praise is very important, and they will cooperate to get it. They are curious, eager to learn, and have stable emotions.

Six-year-olds start to lose their baby teeth and grow permanent ones, have proportions similar to those of an adult, need lots of opportunity to move, can sometimes ride bicycles, and have a preference for using their right or left hands. Their emotions are very near the surface; in fact, they can be puzzled and alarmed by their own yo-yo feelings. They often become bossy and like to make rules and have them obeyed—by others.

These children can reflect on the past and future, want to know about their parents' past (although the sequence of events means little), can take on and complete small chores, and can think about how one activity will affect another. They sing well and read, often with a finger following the words on the page. They learn that others have rights too, and they begin to express their emotions in socially accepted ways.

SPIRITUAL DEVELOPMENT

Ages five to six are an important time of learning about relationships and how they work, both with God and with people. Now is when they need to establish a strong foundational understanding of why relationships are so important and how they affect themselves, others, and their daily lives and interactions.

Children this age are no longer so passive. They are ready to be pulled into active involvement in their own development. It's important for them to learn that it is not just your relationship with God—it's theirs. So they can, for example, begin to say their own prayers, and they need to read regularly from their Bible storybooks with you.

At this age, expect that children will want to do other things rather than pray, read the Bible, and so on. This is normal. When given the choice between work and learning or fun and relaxation, they'll often pick the latter (as will many adults!). How do you handle this? Be careful not to make learning about God seem like work—something you have to do but would like to get done with. Your own positive attitude will help enormously here. When you read Bible stories to your children or pray with them, give them your full and undivided attention. If they have questions or comments, listen to them. If something bothers them, take the time to talk about it and pray about it. Don't let what you planned to do become so rigid that you can't shift gears when needed. This is how God listens to us, and this is how we can model to our kids that God listens.

> Ages five to six are an important time of learning about relationships and how they work, both with God and with people.

KEY WAYS TO PREPARE THEIR RESPONSE

At this stage growing autonomy is the name of the game. If their life snapshots until now have always included you front and center, now they're starting to include their friends and growing social contacts—often with you in the background. The key is to make those snapshots positive pictures.

Talk about how they like to be treated. Keep in mind that children have to be taught how to have relationships with God and others. They need to learn what acceptable treatment of others is, how to talk nicely, how to share, when to apologize and why. They need to learn to respect others and their wills, rights, and property. They need to learn it all from someone—you. Similarly, they have to learn how to develop a relationship with God through prayer, worship, reading His Word, and learning to trust and follow Him. As you teach them, remember that they are unique. Be sensitive to their individual characters and development.

Use your relationship with them. You are developing your own unique relationship and rapport with your children as their personalities become evident and more defined. You're beginning to know who they are. Use this rapport and love to show them what a relationship with God is like. For example, help them see that if they never talked to you, or vice versa, you wouldn't know each other very well, nor would you be able to meet their needs properly. It's the same with God.

Remember to keep the focus on relationship. The relationship your children establish here with God will be with them for the rest of their lives. It's important to establish the right basis for it: love, concern, active care, and interest. For example, when they are worried about monsters under the bed, remind them that God cares for them—they can trust Him.

Have them start saying their own prayers. Until now you have been praying over them or saying their prayers for them. They need to move increasingly into making their prayers their own. You can still help them decide what to pray for, but now they can pray for the things on their list in their own words. As they grow in this, you could alternate—one night you pray, the next they do, gradually increasing the nights they do it.

Talk about reasons for obeying. Children have already been working on obeying you; now they can understand that they obey because of their relationship with God—He wants them to. Let them know that you have to obey too: You have to obey God, your boss at work, etc. Explain how cooperation and obedience make things work better. And always give them the reason for obedience: because God loves them and knows what's best. He tells them to do things that will benefit them and others around them. This keeps God from becoming the "heavy" or the disciplinarian in the sky. Focus rather on the good things about God: His love for them, His ability and willingness to care for them, His desire for their best.

COMMON REFLECTIONS OF FAITH AT THIS AGE

When your children are ready to move on to the next stage, they will have a solid foundation of the bigger picture of the Bible and a relationship with God and will begin to see how the pieces fit together. They will understand that life is all about relationship: between God and them and between them and others. They'll have basic social and spiritual skills and will be ready to learn more.

Remember the "Memory Marker" of your children's dedications—a first step in their faith journeys that they can always think back to. That one, of course, is a memory they'll have only from photographs and your memory of the day. A Memory Marker for this stage of their development is a deciding point where you make sure your child understands the basic gospel (good news) message about salvation through Jesus and then your child chooses to accept Jesus as Savior and Lord.

> When you make God a natural, consistent part of your lives, developing a relationship with Him will come easily for your children.

If you've been reading Bible storybooks, your children will start to understand the context of how their relationship with God fits into life. As their knowledge of Jesus grows, they will be able to grasp the simple message of their relationship with God being broken because of sin; of Jesus, God's Son, dying in their place; of their need to accept what Jesus did; and of living with Him forever.

Respond to their curiosity about accepting Jesus. Since they won't become curious about information they don't have, use a variety of stories, situations, and media to talk about salvation. Use times like Christmas and Easter or church baptisms to reinforce the story and expand their knowledge. When they know Jesus died on the cross, they'll want to know why. What a great opportunity to help them understand salvation!

Your kindergarten-aged child won't understand every aspect of doctrine or of what following God for life is going to mean, but many children ask Jesus into their hearts at this age or younger. The Spirit of God draws them to Himself, and He knows when they're ready—and He will keep drawing them throughout their lives. Jesus said, "Let the little children come to me, and do not hinder them, for the kingdom of heaven belongs to such as these" (Matthew 19:14). He also quoted Psalm 8:2: "From the lips of children and infants you have ordained praise" (Matthew 21:16). And finally, there can be great wisdom in the simplicity of a child's understanding of the "deep things of God"!

THE THINGS ABOUT GOD THEY'RE READY TO LEARN

This chart shows the information your children are ready to learn during this stage. In each area, topics that they can grasp are listed. If it seems like a lot of truth for such small children to be learning, remember how absorbent these young minds are—and remember how much they learned from zero to four! The chapters that follow in this section will help you incorporate all these concepts into your children's agenda for spiritual learning during this stage of five to six.

Ages 5–6

KNOWING		LOVING	LOVING	
A. Who God Is	B. What God Has Done	C. You Can Have a Relationship with God	D. You Can Be All God Wants You to Be	E. You Can Do All God Wants You to Do
1. God is your loving Father. He wants to guide, teach, love, protect, and provide for you. 2. In some ways, you are just like God. He has feelings and thoughts. He can understand you. Jesus showed us who God is and what He's like. 3. In other ways, you are very different from God. He is everywhere; He can do anything; and He knows everything. 4. Jesus has always been with God and is God.	5. God tells you about Himself, His Son, Jesus, and His plan for you in the Bible: The One Big Story. 6. God sent His Son, Jesus Christ, to die for you. 7. God has prepared a place for you in heaven. Jesus is coming back for you.	8. You can have a relationship with God by accepting what Jesus did for you: Salvation. 9. God wants to have a relationship with you. 10. You can talk to God through prayer. 11. You can thank God for all He has done and still does for you. 12. You can ask God for wisdom and guidance. 13. You can read about God and His Son, Jesus, in the Bible or in a Bible storybook. You can begin to have personal Bible reading and time with God.	14. God has a plan for you. 15. The Bible tells you the kind of person God wants you to be. 16. God's way works best. You can be all God wants you to be by following Jesus. 17. God wants you to put only good things into your heart. 18. When you sin, you should ask God to forgive you—and He will.	19. God wants you to spend time with other Christians, both at church and in the community. 20. God wants you to help others and be nice to them. 21. God wants you to obey Him and follow Jesus in everything. 22. God wants you to share and take good care of everything He gives you: Stewardship. 23. God wants you to understand and memorize Bible verses.

CHAPTER 6

— — — — — — — —

Knowing

What Your 5–6-Year-Old Can Learn about God's Character and Actions

In this era of growing relationships, it will be important to keep building on to the earlier truths your child learned about who God is (His character and personality) and what God has done.

LEARNING MORE ABOUT WHO GOD IS

GOD IS YOUR LOVING FATHER.

Children need to understand what "God is your loving Father" means in practical terms. You're probably already demonstrating that every loving parent wants to take care of his or her children, guide them, protect them, teach them, help them grow strong and wise, clothe and feed them, give them advice, help them with homework, and more.

Explain to your children that God, their heavenly Father, wants all this for them too. He made them because He wants a loving relationship with them. As you make it clear that God is loving, children will see Him as approachable and want to move closer to Him.

Show your child James 1:17, and talk about God's consistency and

His unchanging goodness: "Every good and perfect gift is from above, coming down from the Father of the heavenly lights, who does not change like shifting shadows."

Emphasize with your child the most prominent characteristic of God: that He is love: "How great is the love the Father has lavished on us, that we should be called children of God! And that is what we are!" (1 John 3:1).

When your child needs something, involve God in the equation if possible. For example, if your child asks for a glass of milk, you might mention how wonderful it is that God made cows and helped people make dairy farms and grocery stores. If your child is worried about a sick pet or having trouble breaking a bad habit, pray together about that.

> Have fun exploring the created uniqueness of your children. Help them to connect their talents and personalities with God's character.

At gift-giving times—Christmas and birthdays, for instance—remind your children that every good thing ultimately comes from God and that He enjoys giving it to them. This doesn't mean that human gift-givers shouldn't get credit; it may mean sending thank-you prayers as well as thank-you notes.

When your children are ill or injured, assure them that God cares—even if He doesn't answer requests for healing right away. You may want to tell the story of how Jesus didn't heal Lazarus immediately, how Jesus cried when He saw how hard the death of Lazarus was on His friends, and how Jesus finally raised Lazarus to life (John 11:1-44).

IN SOME WAYS YOU ARE JUST LIKE GOD.

Your children are like God in some ways because God made people in His image: "Then God said, 'Let us make man in our image, in our likeness.' . . . So God created man in his own image, in the image of God he created him; male and female he created them" (Genesis 1:26-27). Inform your children that, like them, God feels emotions like sadness, anger, and joy; He also laughs, talks, thinks, makes things, and forms friendships. Comprehending their "likeness to God" is important to children because it lets them know that God understands them and can help them. It also makes God more real to them—easier to believe in, relate to, and talk with.

Your children can perhaps relate to Jesus even more easily because Jesus was a flesh-and-blood human whose activities and choices are recorded for them to read. Your child can relate to Jesus, who felt the same feelings and temptations that they experience: "Since the children have flesh and blood, he too shared in their humanity. . . . Because he himself suffered when he was tempted, he is able to help those who are being tempted" (Hebrews 2:14, 18).

Have fun exploring the created uniqueness of your children. Help them to connect their talents and personalities with God's character. You might schedule a family talent show. Let each child demonstrate an ability—anything from playing the piano to making funny faces. Afterward, talk about God's "talents." Which ones has He "passed on" to humans (compassion, capacity to forgive, creativity, joy)? Which ones has He reserved for Himself (omnipotence, sovereignty, omniscience)?

During an upcoming meal, make God your guest. You may even want to set a place for Him as a reminder to your children that He's always there. As you laugh together, thank God for fun. When you mention how proud you are of your children, tell them God is too. When they tell jokes, remind them that God has a sense of humor as well.

Take your children out one at a time for lunch, dinner, miniature golf, or another activity. As you talk and listen, affirm your interest in your children's lives. Then let them know that God enjoys them too. Remind them that God is thinking about them and likes being with them.

IN OTHER WAYS YOU ARE VERY DIFFERENT FROM GOD.
Though we're made in God's image, we certainly aren't His equals. Let your children know that, unlike us, God can do anything, knows everything, and is everywhere. Nothing is too hard for Him to do or too small for Him to bother with; there is nothing He doesn't understand; no place is out of His reach. Understanding these truths will help your children trust God when the world seems scary, confusing, or out of control.

WORDS ABOUT PRAYER

If you're talking to your child about prayer, consider reading or discussing some of the following verses that show how God feels about our requests:

- John 14:13-14 ("And I will do whatever you ask in my name, so that the Son may bring glory to the Father. You may ask me for anything in my name, and I will do it.")

- Romans 8:31-32 ("If God is for us, who can be against us? He who did not spare his own Son, but gave him up for us all—how will he not also, along with him, graciously give us all things?")

- Matthew 7:7-11 ("Ask and it will be given to you; seek and you will find; knock and the door will be opened to you. For everyone who asks receives; he who seeks finds; and to him who knocks, the door will be opened. Which of you, if his son asks for bread, will give him a stone? Or if he asks for a fish, will give him a snake? If you, then, though you are evil, know how to give good gifts to your children, how much more will your Father in heaven give good gifts to those who ask him!")

- Ephesians 3:20-21 ("Now to him who is able to do immeasurably more than all we ask or imagine, according to his power that is at work within us, to him be glory in the church and in Christ Jesus throughout all generations, for ever and ever!")

Take time to explore Bible texts that discuss God's ultimate power: "Ah, Sovereign Lord, you have made the heavens and the earth by your great power and outstretched arm. Nothing is too hard for you" (Jeremiah 32:17).

Talk about the ways people are limited, but that God can do anything: "With man this is impossible, but with God all things are possible" (Matthew 19:26). Remind your children that God knows everything: "Great is our Lord and mighty in power; his understanding has no limit" (Psalm 147:5) and "Even the very hairs of your head are all numbered" (Matthew 10:30). Inform your children that no one and nothing can be hidden from God (see Jeremiah 23:24).

At this stage children are beginning to discover the vastness of God's creation. They often develop an interest in the solar system, volcanoes, dinosaurs, the undersea world, and other big things God has made. Check out library books and videos that describe the awesome size of Jupiter, the mind-boggling distances between stars, the depth of the seas. Look together at maps and globes that show how large countries and continents are. As you do, talk about how powerful God must be to make such gigantic things.

Assure your children that they can ask God for big things. He can handle anything. Hinting that there are some requests they shouldn't make sows doubt and undermines trust. *But what if my kids want it to snow in the middle of summer?* you might wonder. Let them ask! They need to learn to go to God for everything—and trust Him to do what's best. Explain that sometimes this means His answer will be no—just as sometimes you, too, say no because a thing's not good for them, because the time isn't right, or because you have a better plan.

If you've been disappointed by seemingly unanswered prayer, it may be difficult for you to assure your children that God can do anything. You may worry that by doing so you will be setting them up for disappointment, too. Let your children know that you are learning to trust God. Go to the Bible with them and look up verses about God's attitude toward our requests (see sidebar on page 44 for ideas). Spend time meditating on how God is different from you, on how big and powerful He is. Discuss your feelings with a pastor or mature Christian friend if you like. As you gain confidence in God's power, you'll be better able to teach your children trust—in His willingness to answer as well as the wisdom of His responses.

JESUS HAS ALWAYS BEEN WITH GOD AND IS GOD.

The Jesus most children relate to is the Man, their Friend. But they also need to know that He is God, with all the same qualities and abilities as God the Father. He was always alive and with God from before time began. He made everything: "In the beginning was the Word, and the Word was with God, and the Word was God. He was with God in the beginning. Through him all things were made; without him nothing was made that has been made" (John 1:1-3; "the Word" is Jesus; see also

John 1:14). When children know that Jesus made everything and therefore knows how it all works, they understand that He knows the very best way to live.

When possible, as you read your children Bible stories about Jesus or talk about Him during the course of a day, try to convey the awesomeness of who He is: God the Son, who has always been, who created everything. For instance, while telling the story of how Jesus fed thousands of people, you might say, "Making a big meal out of a few loaves and fish was no trouble for Jesus—He made all the fish in the ocean!" Or, when talking about how Jesus blessed the children, you could ask, "If you were standing in line to see Jesus, would you be nervous? Do you think those children knew that He is God?" Such side notes of awe, wonder, and respect help your children begin to understand the divine nature of Jesus. It's easy to stop being wowed by who He is and what He did. Remind yourself and convey the "wow" to your children!

At Christmas, our celebrations often emphasize the human side of Jesus—the vulnerable baby in the manger. If you want to remind your children that Jesus is also God, an Advent calendar may help. As your children open a little door on the calendar each day during December, wonder together what might have been going on in heaven as God's Son prepared to come to earth in human form.

LEARNING MORE ABOUT WHAT GOD HAS DONE

GOD TELLS YOU ABOUT HIMSELF, HIS SON, JESUS, AND HIS PLAN FOR YOU IN THE BIBLE.

Once your children know the Bible is God's book, they need to learn why He gave it to them. Let them know that through the Bible they can find out about the God who loves them so much and about His plan for them. It's their instruction manual for life: "Your word is a lamp to my feet and a light for my path" (Psalm 119:105). And their personal instruction book was prepared by the inventor of life Himself: "All Scripture is God-breathed and is useful for teaching, rebuking, correcting and training in righteousness, so that the man of God may be thoroughly equipped for every good work" (2 Timothy 3:16-17).

The Bible is a love letter! It's an autobiography! It's a history book! It's a true adventure! Refer to the Bible in a variety of ways so that your children can see that it has a number of purposes. Bring out the instruction book to your VCR, camera, or other device. Explain that the book helps you know how the device works best and how to get the most from it. Point out that the Bible is our instruction book for life, written by the God who created us. You can do the same thing with other kinds of books—an encyclopedia, where we look up answers to our questions; an atlas, which shows us which way to go on a trip; and so on.

No matter how many Bibles or Bible storybooks you may have in your home, be sure that each child sees a particular one as belonging to him or her. Your children need "personal" Bibles or Bible storybooks. This reinforces the idea that God's special book is for them.

If your Bible storybook doesn't link the stories together, try doing this yourself as you read them. Help children understand the order of the stories—for example, that Adam and Eve came before Noah, who came before Abraham, who came before David, who came before Jesus. This adds to your children's understanding of the overall story. So does learning the names and order of the books of the Bible, which children can begin to do at this age.

Children need to know that even though the Bible is made up of many stories, they add up to the One Big Story of God's plan for the world from creation to eternity. That plan: to make it possible for us to be His children. Besides giving your children a context for each story, this helps them find their way around the Bible, thereby making it less likely that they'll be intimidated by "big" Bibles later on. (To help your children discover God's overall One Big Story, try reading the version that appears in the appendix of this book.)

> Being forgiven and becoming a Christian is the start of a loving relationship—a foundation on which your children can build throughout their lives.

GOD SENT HIS SON, JESUS CHRIST, TO DIE FOR YOU.

Knowing the facts of Jesus' life, death, and resurrection is vital for your children. But understanding why these things matter to them personally is even more important. You might want to explain it this way to your five-to-six-year-old:

> Jesus was the perfect Person God's plan needed. Since He is God's Son, He is the only Person since Adam's and Eve's first sin ever to be born without sin. He grew up like you, obeying His parents, doing chores, going to school, playing, and learning things. When Jesus was 30, He began the job God had given Him. He traveled around His country telling people what God was like, showing them that God loved them. He was friends with people others avoided, and He welcomed children. Jesus also showed people that God is powerful. He taught them about God's kingdom, how life works, how to pray, and what things are really important. For example, He

said that how you are on the inside is even more important than how you act.

The religious leaders didn't like what Jesus was teaching and doing. They were jealous, so they planned to get rid of Him. They asked Judas, one of Jesus' followers, to help them. One night, when Jesus was talking to His friends, the religious leaders sent Judas with a crowd to arrest Him. They took Him to the ruler of the area and put Him on trial because He said He was God's Son. The ruler tried to free Jesus, but he was afraid of the people and finally gave Jesus to the soldiers to be nailed to a cross and killed.

Jesus had done nothing wrong. He is perfect. He could have stopped the soldiers from killing Him, but He didn't. He didn't need to die at all because He has never sinned. But He died to pay for your sins, and for the sins of everyone who ever lived, so that you could be forgiven and be God's child as God always wanted.

But that's not the end of the story. Jesus didn't stay dead. When He rose from the dead, He showed that God was stronger than death and had accepted His death in place of everyone else's. Jesus told His friends to tell others the truth and then went back into heaven to be with God. One day Jesus will come back for all God's children—those who believe Jesus died for them and who thus have been forgiven. They will all be with God forever. Nothing will ever separate them from God's love again!

To help children understand the meaning of Jesus' sacrifice, you can read the preceding story, read them a good storybook about Jesus' death and resurrection, or show them a video on the subject (be sure to screen the video yourself first to make sure it's appropriate for your children). Show your children the passage in John where Jesus explains how it's possible to be born again: "For God so loved the world that he gave his one and only Son, that whoever believes in him shall not perish but have eternal life" (John 3:16). Answer any questions they have; if you don't know an answer, promise to investigate and get back to them. If you can't find the answer in your Bible or this book, consult your children's Sunday school teacher or your pastor.

When your children appear to understand the basics of what Jesus has done for them, simply ask something like "Do you want to pray and ask God to forgive you and make you His child right now?" Using the phrase "right now" makes it easier for you to ask them again later if they aren't ready yet.

If they are ready, have them pray in their own words or repeat a simple prayer after you, such as this one:

> Dear God, I know that I've done wrong things and sinned. I'm sorry. I know that Jesus, Your Son, died for my sins and rose from the dead. Please forgive me and make me Your child. Help me to trust and obey You and make the right choices. Thank You for loving me and making me Your child. In Jesus' name, amen.

How old should children be when they pray to accept Jesus as Savior? Some children as young as three can do this, though most won't understand fully what they're doing. If you're concerned that your child has "prayed the prayer" without grasping all the theology, remember that children need only understand the main points. Being forgiven and becoming a Christian is not like signing a contract when you must be careful to read all the fine print. It is the start of a loving relationship—a foundation on which your children can build throughout their lives.

If your children don't accept Jesus in exactly the same way or setting as you might have envisioned, try not to worry or be disappointed. There is no single "correct" way to come to Jesus. It can happen with you, in church or Sunday school, with a friend, as children are thinking by themselves—anywhere. It might be emotional or matter-of-fact. God wants a unique relationship with each person, and each relationship starts in its own way.

Celebrate with your children when they take Jesus into their hearts: "There is rejoicing in the presence of the angels of God over one sinner who repents" (Luke 15:10). Throw a party! Make it a special occasion to be remembered and treasured—this is a Memory Marker in the spiritual life of your children. This can be a "snapshot" your child will have in his or her "photo album" forever.

GOD HAS PREPARED A PLACE FOR YOU IN HEAVEN; JESUS IS COMING BACK FOR YOU.

Jesus is coming back! The how and when is not as important as the fact of His return. For children, the key is the reason He's returning: to take them to be with Him in heaven forever. Tell your children that Jesus is getting a wonderful place ready for them, looking forward to the time they will be with Him there. It's a place so wonderful, we can't even imagine it: "No eye has seen, no ear has heard, no mind has conceived what God has prepared for those who love him" (1 Corinthians 2:9). When you teach your children about what's ahead for them in heaven, you give them hope—and the beginning of an eternal view that puts things here in perspective. (See also Isaiah 35:10; John 14:2-3; and Revelation 21:3-4.)

People often have the idea that heaven is a boring, static place where nothing ever happens and everyone sits around playing harps. If your children have gotten this impression from TV or other sources, they may wonder, *Why would anyone want to go there?* But heaven will be fantastic! The Bible says there will be no crying, no sadness, no pain or hurt. And heaven isn't just the absence of bad things; the apostle Paul wrote that it's far greater than anyone can even imagine. Next time you and your children enjoy an especially delicious meal, thrilling game, or breath-taking view, point out that heaven is even better.

If your discussion of heaven brings up questions about angels, explain to your children that angels live in heaven and are God's helpers. They carry out God's plans and sometimes deliver His messages (as Gabriel did to Mary and Joseph), and God has them look after Christians. For more about angels, see Psalm 104:4 and Hebrews 1:14.

CHAPTER 7

- - - - - - - - -

Loving

Your 5–6-Year-Old's Relationship with God

These are exciting times in the spiritual life of a child! When children reach five or six, they are able to reach out for a relationship with God—and discover that He is eager for a relationship with them, too!

REACHING FOR A RELATIONSHIP WITH GOD

YOU CAN HAVE A RELATIONSHIP WITH GOD BY ACCEPTING WHAT JESUS DID FOR YOU.

Yes, Jesus died for your children so that their sins could be forgiven. But why? So that they could have a close relationship with God, their heavenly Father: "Jesus answered, 'I am the way and the truth and the life. No one comes to the Father except through me. If you really knew me, you would know my Father as well. From now on, you do know him and have seen him' " (John 14:6-7).

Make sure your children know that God is eager to have a relationship with them. He wants a special friendship with them, one He can have with no one else because each child is one of a kind. In this private relationship they get to know God in their own unique way.

Children need to know that deciding to accept Jesus as Savior is the beginning, not the end. Getting to know God is something exciting they'll be doing for the rest of their lives: "Jesus replied, 'If anyone loves me, he will obey my teaching. My Father will love him, and we will come to him and make our home with him'" (John 14:23).

> **Children need to know that deciding to accept Jesus as Savior is the beginning, not the end. Getting to know God is something exciting they'll be doing for the rest of their lives.**

Let your children see how *your* relationship with God works. Allow them to hear you pray honestly and conversationally; encourage them to pray the same way, even about things that may seem trivial. Tell them about something God has taught you from the Bible. Talk about times when you've felt especially close to God. If you sometimes feel far from Him, admit it; if it's sometimes hard to relate to a person who's invisible and doesn't speak to you audibly, admit that, too. Tell them what you would miss most if you couldn't have a relationship with God. As children learn that a relationship with God can be very real even if it has ups and downs, they'll have more realistic expectations as they begin their own.

Create visual reminders of the relationship between your children and God. Have children draw pictures of themselves hiking with Jesus, for example. Or cut a picture of Jesus from a Sunday school paper and add it to a family portrait. Post these reminders where your children will see them frequently.

GOD WANTS TO HAVE A RELATIONSHIP WITH YOU. YOU CAN TALK TO GOD THROUGH PRAYER.

It's hard to have closeness without communication. Let your children know that the number-one way to develop their relationship with God is through prayer. Explain that because God cares so much for them, He wants to know all the things on their hearts and minds: "Cast all your anxiety on him because he cares for you" (1 Peter 5:7).

At this age they may pray mostly in your presence, at your suggestion. As they move through this stage, however, your goal will be to teach them how to say their own prayers all by themselves: "When you pray, go into your room, close the door and pray to your Father, who is unseen. Then your Father, who sees what is done in secret, will reward you" (Matthew 6:6).

At the start of this stage, depending on your child, you may simply have him or her repeat prayers after you. Or try "Ping-Pong prayers"—you pray something, then the child does, then you do, and so on. Or use "starter prayers"—after you and your child compile a list of things to pray for, you give a one- or two-word clue of something on the list and your child prays about it. This progression will comfortably move children toward saying their own prayers.

As this stage begins, you may be telling your children what to pray about—especially if they have trouble coming up with ideas. Try to make a gradual transition, however, to letting them decide what to talk to God about. Help them make a list by asking questions or making suggestions. Eventually they'll be able to make their own list with a little help. This transfer of responsibility helps them see that this is their relationship with God, not yours.

Variety is the spice of a prayer life, too! Even if your main prayer time is always at bedtime, avoid praying for the same things or in the same way every night. Make each night's prayer as relevant to the day's events as possible. Ask your child to pray for your concerns sometimes. Rearrange the bedtime routine occasionally so that prayer isn't just another step toward "lights out." This reinforces the truth that prayer is meant to be meaningful.

HOW CAN WE TALK TO SOMEONE WE CAN'T SEE?

If your children have difficulty with this, help them understand by standing near them and having them close their eyes. Be quiet for a moment. Then ask, "Am I still here when your eyes are closed? How do you know?" Then explain, "It's like that with God. Even though you can't see Him, you'll know with your heart that He is there. You can know He never left because the Bible says He'll always be with you."

Encourage your children to be themselves with God. There's a difference between respect and the form of respect. Respect is a matter of the heart, not of the words. Speaking in reverent tones and terms might sound respectful, but God sees the heart. He is much more interested in an honest relationship than in a pious-sounding one.

YOU CAN THANK GOD FOR ALL HE HAS DONE AND STILL DOES FOR YOU.

Helping your children to be thankful is one of the greatest gifts you can give them. Thankfulness readies them to receive God's grace, coaches them to expect God's provision and care, and strengthens their faith. An attitude of gratitude leads them to contentment and peace. Being able to recognize blessings in all their forms, large and small, will shape your children's lives and increase their happiness. When Paul exhorted the Philippian Christians to keep praying, he included *thanksgiving*: "Do not be anxious about anything, but in everything, by prayer and petition, *with thanksgiving,* present your requests to God" (Philippians 4:6, emphasis added).

Encouraging your children to notice and thank God for what He's doing will help grow contentment in their hearts (see Philippians 4:12).

Since they think in concrete terms, children don't always make the connection between their prayers and God's answers. Nor do they always link God with the wonderful things they have. Encourage your children to make a list of their Top-10 favorite things; point out that these are gifts from God. If you keep a prayer list, help children to keep track of God's answers, too.

From time to time, at the end of an uneventful day, talk with your child about the not-so-good things that could have happened that day but didn't—getting sick, falling down on the ice, losing milk money on the way to school, being in an earthquake, etc. Thank God together that these things didn't happen.

Let children see your own thankfulness and that you credit your own blessings to God. At mealtime, for example, thank God for more than the food. Modeling gratitude and contentment with what you have gives your children a positive example to follow.

> **Helping your children to be thankful is one of the greatest gifts you can give them. Being able to recognize blessings in all their forms, large and small, will shape your children's lives and increase their happiness.**

YOU CAN ASK GOD FOR WISDOM AND GUIDANCE.

God wants your children to ask for wisdom—the ability to know the right thing to do in a situation. He has all the wisdom they could ever need! Encourage your children to ask for wisdom on a regular basis during prayer time—and anytime they need to know what to do: "If any of you lacks wisdom, he should ask God, who gives generously to all without finding fault, and it will be given to him" (James 1:5; see also 3:15-17). God promises to provide guidance whenever His children ask Him: "If you call out for insight and cry aloud for understanding, and if you look for it as for silver and search for it as for hidden treasure, then you will understand the fear of the LORD and find the knowledge of God" (Proverbs 2:3-5).

Use your children's questions and frustrations as an opportunity to teach them how to ask for God's wisdom. If they're upset about not being able to take a toy apart or put it back together, remind them that

God is ready to help. Show them how to stop and be still for a moment while they ask God for wisdom. Help them think through their situation and watch the ideas come. If God seems to lead them to ask someone else for help, that's fine. God provides us with wisdom in many different ways and in His time.

Avoid giving your children the answer yourself every time they need guidance. Sometimes it's good to show your children how to do something, but at other times you can take them to God for wisdom. They need to know what to do when you're not around. So take the time to walk them through a process of thinking and praying that they can use when you're not there.

YOU CAN READ ABOUT GOD AND HIS SON, JESUS, IN THE BIBLE OR A BIBLE STORYBOOK; YOU CAN HAVE PERSONAL BIBLE READING AND TIME WITH GOD.

It's time to take Bible reading to another level. Let your children know that God can teach them things as they read: "These are the Scriptures that testify about me" (John 5:39). When you sit down to read together, get in the habit of quickly asking God, with your child, to help you learn from and understand His Word before you read it. Perhaps you could read Psalm 119 with your child, searching out all the verses that praise and value the "law" (God's Word).

From time to time, mention to your children that eventually they'll read the Bible on their own. Help them look forward to this as part of being a "big kid"—and part of spending time with God daily and getting to know Him better. At this point you probably will read with them, but let them take some initiative. For instance, they can get their Bible storybook and put it away, place the bookmark when you're done, and help to decide whether you read one, two, or three stories at a time.

As you read, you may be amazed at how often something in a Bible story coincides with your children's current struggles or even with what happened that day. Talk to your children about the parallel. Show them how what happened in the story compares with what happened in their

day. This helps them see how relevant the Bible is and how God uses it to speak to them.

Look for opportunities to work a Bible story's truths into your child's prayer time. For example, you might pray, "God, please help Jeannie trust You the way David trusted You with Goliath." This affirms that Bible lessons are for applying, and that we can trust God to help us change as we learn from His Word.

CHAPTER 8

Living

How 5–6-Year-Olds Can Live Out Their Faith

In the previous section of this book, we talked about how all believers, of every age, live out their faith by *being* God-followers and *doing* what pleases God. Your kindergarten-aged child is ready to move ahead in both of these significant areas.

BEING ALL GOD WANTS YOU TO BE

GOD HAS A PLAN FOR YOU.

God cares not only what your children are like now but also about the people they're going to be. He cares about what they're going to do with their lives. Assure them that they're special to God and that He has a plan for their lives that suits them perfectly. The Creator made your children marvelously: "I praise you because I am fearfully and wonderfully made; your works are wonderful, I know that full well. My frame was not hidden from you when I was made in the secret place. When I was woven together in the depths of the earth, your eyes saw my unformed body. All the days ordained for me were written in your book before one of them came to be" (Psalm 139:14-16). And the Creator had a reason for creating your children: "For we are God's workmanship, created in Christ Jesus to do good works, which God prepared in advance for us to do" (Ephesians 2:10).

Most children love to hear stories about what it was like when they were born and what they did when they were babies. When you speak of events surrounding your children's births, include God's involvement in the story. He was not an absentee Father; He was there, involved in their creation and eagerly awaiting their entry into His world.

> Assure them that they're special to God and that He has a plan for their lives that suits them perfectly.

Take time to dream about the future with your children. Ask, "What would you like to be when you grow up? How could you help other people in a way that maybe no one else could?" Plant the idea that God has a plan for them. Remind them that God wants them to be all they can be, and He will help them do that.

Children need to feel wanted. It's a good foundation for building a sense of purpose, too. You can help children know that both you and God want them, that you're excited they're in the world. You can remind them of this anytime, but birthdays are an especially good time to do so. When you say, "I'm so glad you were born," mention that God is glad too.

THE BIBLE TELLS YOU THE KIND OF PERSON GOD WANTS YOU TO BE. Even young children can understand that the Bible is the most important book they'll ever read—because it explains how life works, what God is like, and how He wants them to be. Explain that the Bible stories and verses help them learn how to please God: "All Scripture is God-breathed and is useful for teaching, rebuking, correcting and training in righteousness, so that the man of God may be thoroughly equipped for every good work" (2 Timothy 3:16-17).

Is your child afraid of a bully at school? Read and discuss the story of

Daniel in the lions' den (Daniel 6). Is your child refusing to forgive someone? Talk about the parable of the unmerciful servant (Matthew 18:21-35). When your children struggle with stress or character issues, remind them of Bible stories that can help them understand how God wants them to be and behave in those situations. This reinforces how relevant God's Word is and that God cares how they feel and act.

Let your children know about an issue with which you struggle—controlling your temper, being generous, trusting God, etc. Show them how you can look in the Bible (starting with a concordance) to find verses that will help you in that area. Let them see you write a few of the verses on index cards; post these where you'll encounter them often. Give children a report every week or so on how God's Word is enabling you to make progress with your problem. At the end of a month, help your children go through a similar process with difficulties they face.

GOD'S WAY WORKS BEST. YOU CAN BE ALL GOD WANTS YOU TO BE BY FOLLOWING JESUS.

God must have known kids would need a practical, concrete motivation to follow His way, so He had Paul put it into words. He told children to obey their parents so that it would go well with them and they would enjoy long life: "Children, obey your parents in the Lord, for this is right. 'Honor your father and mother'—which is the first commandment with a promise—'that it may go well with you and that you may enjoy long life on the earth' " (Ephesians 6:1-3). If your children know and trust God and learn to do things His way, they'll have what they need to get through life instead of being plowed under by it.

God also knew they needed an example. So Jesus lived God's way, and His story in the Bible shows your children how God wants them to act: "I have told you these things, so that in me you may have peace. In this world you will have trouble. But take heart! I have overcome the world" (John 16:33).

When using Bible stories to show how to live God's way, help your children make the connection between the Bible characters' acts and the results. For example, Joseph was faithful to God. He suffered for a time in prison, but later God rewarded his faithfulness, making Joseph the second most important man in Egypt. Jonah illustrates the negative consequences of doing things your own way. Other stories that show consequences clearly are those of King Saul, Gideon, and Pharaoh and the plagues. The stories of Jesus, meanwhile, show the right way to live.

> **If your children know and trust God and learn to do things His way, they'll have what they need to get through life instead of being plowed under by it.**

It's easy when you're tense or hurried to answer your children's questions with "Because I said so." But this reasoning doesn't help them understand that your instructions are for their own good; it doesn't help them trust you. In the same way, "Because God says so" is inadequate. God doesn't just tell us what to do in the Bible; He often tells us why. If you don't know the why behind a command, look it up—or ask someone who knows the Bible better.

GOD WANTS YOU TO PUT ONLY GOOD THINGS INTO YOUR HEART.

Children at this age are starting to watch more TV shows and videos. It's important to teach them early the concept of guarding their hearts. You might say something like "Guarding your heart means being careful about what goes into it. God wants you to choose good things to put into your heart so that you'll be happy." Remind them that, as God is good and kind and loving, we want to be that way too. As a result, we want to watch things that are good and kind and loving: "The good man brings good things out of the good stored up in his heart, and the evil man brings evil things out of the evil stored up in his heart. For out of the overflow of his heart his mouth speaks" (Luke 6:45).

The apostle Paul offered a checklist for the types of things that

should occupy our time and attention: "Finally, brothe
true, whatever is noble, whatever is right, whatever is pu
lovely, whatever is admirable—if anything is excell
worthy—think about such things" (Philippians 4:8).

Wondering how TV, books, and other media are ir
kids? Children's "pretend" play is an excellent window in
Watch what they pretend and you'll see what has gone into
they pick up action figures and "battle" to the death? Do t
"talk" harshly to each other, or about inappropriately "adult"
can trace these behaviors back to specific shows or other
whether you need to make those sources off-limits—and ex

Children this age can be fearful and have nightmare
they're getting the wrong input. Explain to your children t
have bad dreams, it may be the result of watching thing
them. Comfort and pray for them first, then try to help
the source of their fears. Let them know that if they want
they need to put good things into their hearts.

Are your children bothered by minor violence, scar
words in TV shows or movies? Instead of implying that
praise them for being sensitive. Help them make the dec
away from such sights and sounds.

Be careful not to set a double standard in your home,
fect, "You can't watch certain things, but I can watch anyt
I'm an adult." Show your children that you also put limits
watch in order to guard your heart and please God.

WHEN YOU SIN, YOU SHOULD ASK GOD TO FORGIVE YO
AND HE WILL.

It's important to teach children that when they willfully disc
do something wrong, they need to ask God to forgive ther
need to ask whoever else was involved to forgive them. Thi
learn the difference between right and wrong and reinforces
to do what is right.

Often children (and adults) can get caught up in making similar
stakes repeatedly. They need to come to a point of conscious choice
ere they say, "I will not be that way or do that anymore!" Repentance
ps them do this. When they stop for a time-out after bad behavior,
k to them about forgiveness, telling them the following two things:
st, when they repent and ask for forgiveness, they are making a deci-
n to leave that behavior behind and asking God for help to do it right
m now on. Second, God wants them to learn to do right because He
nts them to have a good life. So when they ask for forgiveness, God
tantly forgives them: "If we confess our sins, he is faithful and just and
ll forgive us our sins and purify us from all unrighteousness" (1 John
). They start again with a clean slate.

After correcting your children, show them what they could have
ne instead. For example, if your child breaks something and then de-
s it or lies about it, explain that you are more upset with the lie than
th the fact that the object is broken. Gently tell them what the proper
sponse would have been—they should have come to you and simply
plained what happened. Then you would have had only the accident
deal with, not the issue of the lie.

Make sure, once you've talked about the sin and prayed about it, that
u don't harp on it anymore. Represent God to your children: hug them
d tell them how much you love them, how pleased you are generally
th their behavior, and how pleased you are with how they responded.

When your children are asking for forgiveness from God, they
ight be uncomfortable because they feel so bad. In this case it's a good
ea for you to pray for them. Keep it short and simple: ask God to for-
ve them and teach them, and thank Him for some good things about
ur children that you enjoy.

OING ALL GOD WANTS YOU TO DO

OD WANTS YOU TO SPEND TIME WITH OTHER CHRISTIANS.

you and your children are involved with peers at church, keep it up! If
t, start now. Relational development is very important in this stage.

Teach your children the difference between, on one hand, loving and being friendly with everyone, and on the other hand, finding good friends that they will want to spend a lot of time with. The Bible teaches that we become like the people we spend time with and get close to: "Do not be misled: 'Bad company corrupts good character' " (1 Corinthians 15:33).

Your children should be involved in a Sunday school class, children's church, or group where they learn about God, Jesus, and the Bible; have a good time; and meet people who can become good friends. Help them meet other adult Christians who can be mentors to them: "And let us consider how we may spur one another on toward love and good deeds. Let us not give up meeting together, as some are in the habit of doing, but let us encourage one another—and all the more as you see the Day approaching" (Hebrews 10:24-25).

You can't choose your children's friends; after all, they may not click with the same personality types you do. But you can choose the environment from which they take their friends. Make it easy for them to spend time with Christian children. Drive them to church events, have Christian children over, encourage return visits.

Follow up on the time your children spend at church. Discuss what they learned and sang and what their favorite parts were. Many Sunday schools send home papers and memory verses; if yours does, go over these with your children, making sure they understand the story and lesson. You might even read the same Bible story together during the week. Hanging the Sunday school material and memory verses on the refrigerator or bulletin board may help you remember to review it. This involvement quietly but powerfully demonstrates to your children that church and what they do there is important.

GOD WANTS YOU TO HELP OTHERS AND BE NICE TO THEM— GETTING ALONG WITH OTHERS.

At this age, your children are forming habits of relating and communicating that will be with them the rest of their lives. Now's the time for them to learn to respect other people's bodies, property, space, rights, and feelings. You can teach them to . . .

Respect others' ownership of their own person. A person's body is his or her own, and he or she sets the limits on whether and how he or she  wishes to be touched. How can you teach children about respectful touching? Let's say Michelle is in the way, so brother Sean pushes her roughly. Tell Sean that Michelle's body is hers, and he doesn't have the right to touch her unless she wants him to. Explain that he mustn't push, punch, or pinch. He shouldn't even tickle if she doesn't want it. If she asks him to stop, he must stop. Tell Sean to ask Michelle to please move because he would like to get through. That way Michelle is able to please him without having him touch her without respect.

Respect others' property. When something belongs to someone else, your children cannot use it without permission.

Respect others' personal space. Some people like to get really close, but others need more space. This also applies to going into rooms or looking into cupboards if children haven't been invited.

Respect others' feelings. Children need to be caring and compassionate toward others. Show your children how to respond compassionately to someone—brother, sister, friend—who is hurt or upset. If someone gets hurt during play, blame is usually the first issue. Help children make concern for the hurt or upset person the first issue. As you insist that feelings are dealt with first and apologies are given, blame tends to become a nonissue.

Respect with words. Yelling, being mean, saying cruel things, and calling names are unacceptable. Children need to be gentle, kind, and loving with their words. Explain the long-term benefits of treating others well: growing relationships that are strong and precious because of trust and love; being trusted, loved, and sought after; getting along well at school, on the playing field, with friends, at church, and (later) at work.

Always help your children understand the overarching reason for their respectful interaction with others: "This is his command: to believe in the name of his Son, Jesus Christ, and to love one another as he commanded us" (1 John 3:23). Remind them that we show how much we love God by the way that we love others: "If anyone says, 'I love God,' yet hates his brother, he is a liar. For anyone who does not love his brother, whom he has seen, cannot love God, whom he has not seen" (1 John 4:20).

GOD WANTS YOU TO OBEY HIM AND FOLLOW JESUS IN EVERYTHING.
Your children won't always understand why God says to do something. But if you're teaching them who God is and what His character is like, they'll be more likely to trust that His way is best. Children also need to know that, whether they understand the reason or not, it's vital to obey. Their obedience does not depend on their understanding; He is, after all, God.

Show your children the Bible's emphasis on the link between our love for God and our obedience: "Jesus replied, 'If anyone loves me, he will obey my teaching. My Father will love him, and we will come to him and make our home with him. He who does not love me will not obey my teaching. These words you hear are not my own; they belong to the Father who sent me'" (John 14:23-24). Our obedience keeps our relationship with God clear and direct: "Dear friends, if our hearts do not condemn us, we have confidence before God and receive from him anything we ask, because we obey his commands and do what pleases him" (1 John 3:21-22).

Many children in this stage are fascinated by the human body and how it works. Using age-appropriate books, explore with your children the amazingly intricate way in which God has created us—from our infection-fighting blood cells to our self-mending skin. Point out that God knows everything about us because He made us; we need to respect Him and obey Him simply because He's our Creator.

Talk with your children about how they need to obey you right away, even if they don't understand. They can ask questions after they've obeyed. If they're walking into the street and don't see a car coming, they must obey you immediately when you tell them to stop and come back. That's not the time to debate reasons. They need to trust that you have their best in mind, even if they can't see how obeying will benefit them. It's the same with God.

GOD WANTS YOU TO SHARE AND TAKE GOOD CARE OF EVERYTHING HE GIVES YOU.

God owns absolutely everything: "The earth is the LORD's, and everything in it, the world, and all who live in it" (Psalm 24:1). He made it all! But He gives it to you and your children to use and manage for Him. That's the job of a steward. When you tell your children that everything

they have belongs to God and that they're just stewards of it, get specific: toys, clothes, games, videos, books, money, the natural world around them. They're also stewards of their abilities, time, energy, minds, hearts, relationships with God and people, and hopes for the future. All of these are gifts from God: "For who makes you different from anyone else? What do you have that you did not receive? And if you did receive it, why do you boast as though you did not?" (1 Corinthians 4:7). How should they use these gifts? The way God has shown them to through His example: generously, selflessly, wisely.

Children may resist sharing if they're worried about not having enough left for themselves. Explain that when they obey God by sharing, they don't have to worry about running out. It's God's job to take care of them. Their faith and trust in His care are shown by their willingness to give back to God and to help others.

Are you starting to give your children an allowance? If so, it's a good time to teach them why you give to the church. Explain that you give some of your money back to God as a thank-you for all the wonderful things He's given you. Giving to the church is also a way to show God that you trust Him to look after your needs—and it helps to get God's work done.

Most children in this stage can easily understand what it means to be "stewards" of God's creation—taking care of the environment, not wasting water or other resources, keeping the world clean by not littering, etc. Explain that this applies to all the things God has given us.

Teaching children to be good stewards teaches them other spiritual truths, too. For example, tithing teaches them to be thankful for God's care and to value God's church and the Christian community. Giving to missions teaches them their responsibility to reach those who don't know Jesus.

GOD WANTS YOU TO UNDERSTAND AND MEMORIZE BIBLE VERSES.
Why does the Bible encourage memorizing Scripture? So that God's Word, hidden in children's minds and hearts, can guide them: "Your

MEMORY VERSES

Here are some simple memory verses to try with your child:

- Genesis 1:1
- Proverbs 3:5
- Proverbs 17:17
- Luke 6:31
- John 3:16
- Galatians 5:22-23
- Ephesians 4:2
- Philippians 4:6
- 2 Timothy 1:7

word is a lamp to my feet and a light for my path" (Psalm 119:105). Prizes and rewards can help to motivate memorizing—but if the purpose doesn't go beyond that, kids might as well memorize Shakespeare. It's also more important for children to understand the verses than to have them letter-perfect.

The best verses to memorize are ones you've quoted or looked up together when you helped your children understand one of life's principles. In so doing, you've given them a context that helps make their meaning clear. Help your children understand that memorizing helps you make a verse your own: "Anyone who listens to the word but does not do what it says is like a man who looks at his face in a mirror and, after looking at himself, goes away and immediately forgets what he looks like. But the man who looks intently into the perfect law that gives freedom, and continues to do this, not forgetting what he has heard, but doing it—he will be blessed in what he does" (James 1:23-25).

To help your children memorize a verse with meaning, read it and guide them to think about it. Talk about what it means. Read it again and ask, "When might this verse help you?" Remind children that they want to get the verse's meaning inside, in their thoughts and hearts. Read the verse a few more times, then close the Bible and say it out loud with them. Repeat it with them until they have it. Repetition, not memory concentration, is the key to memorizing at this age. For variety, try using rhythms or songs that make the words stick.

Don't overdo it by giving children too many verses to memorize. And avoid picking verses randomly. Choose a few that reinforce what you've been teaching them lately. For additional ideas, see the sidebar on page 71.

CHART IT!

Your five-to-six-year-old child is on his way, well-launched in knowing who God is, in developing a relationship with God, and in living out his faith. Check out this chart to remind yourself and your child how much you've been learning!

Ages 5–6

KNOWING		LOVING	LIVING	
A. Who God Is	B. What God Has Done	C. You Can Have a Relationship with God	D. You Can Be All God Wants You to Be	E. You Can Do All God Wants You to Do
1. God is your loving Father. He wants to guide, teach, love, protect, and provide for you. 2. In some ways, you are just like God. He has feelings and thoughts. He can understand you. Jesus showed us who God is and what He's like. 3. In other ways, you are very different from God. He is everywhere; He can do anything; and He knows everything. 4. Jesus has always been with God and is God.	5. God tells you about Himself, His Son, Jesus, and His plan for you in the Bible: The One Big Story. 6. God sent His Son, Jesus Christ, to die for you. 7. God has prepared a place for you in heaven. Jesus is coming back for you.	8. You can have a relationship with God by accepting what Jesus did for you: Salvation. 9. God wants to have a relationship with you. 10. You can talk to God through prayer. 11. You can thank God for all He has done and still does for you. 12. You can ask God for wisdom and guidance. 13. You can read about God and His Son, Jesus, in the Bible or in a Bible storybook. You can begin to have personal Bible reading and time with God.	14. God has a plan for you. 15. The Bible tells you the kind of person God wants you to be. 16. God's way works best. You can be all God wants you to be by following Jesus. 17. God wants you to put only good things into your heart. 18. When you sin, you should ask God to forgive you—and He will.	19. God wants you to spend time with other Christians, both at church and in the community. 20. God wants you to help others and be nice to them. 21. God wants you to obey Him and follow Jesus in everything. 22. God wants you to share and take good care of everything He gives you: Stewardship. 23. God wants you to understand and memorize Bible verses.

PART 3

—

From Bikes to Bibles:
What Your 7-9-Year-Old Can Learn about God

Giving Children the Reasons for Their Faith

As they move ahead in their spiritual lives, your children need to know they can trust God and that their relationship with Him rests on His consistent character. They need the assurance that, when they grow up in God's presence with a solid personal relationship with Him, He will be their foundation. Children need to have God's trustworthiness, love, care, and provision reinforced to them. They are now also ready to begin understanding the basis of their faith and to learn the reasons for what they believe.

DEVELOPMENTAL DISTINCTIVES

In this stage, children are beginning to think for themselves. They are ready to understand more and believe more.

PHYSICAL AND MENTAL DEVELOPMENT

Children's forebrains undergo a growth spurt during this stage, so that by age eight their brains are 90 percent of their adult size. They begin to internalize values and integrate moral principles, buying into what you've taught them and developing good habits. Family is still the most important influence, but peer groups are gaining.

Seven is the "eraser age": Children want to do perfect work to gain approval, so they often try to erase their errors. They become more coordinated and graceful (a good time for sports), and they need to overcome being sore losers and telling tales. To children eight and nine, rules are decided by adults and should therefore be kept. Hero worship is big, based on their acceptance of adult authority. They express themselves through writing, enjoy reading, remember several things at once, have a good concept of time (they understand months and years), and remember facts longer. Self-esteem is high: They believe they can do anything they set their minds to.

These children can think systematically and logically; deal with concrete, real ideas; are independent, industrious, and willing to perfect new skills. Friendships form and gender differences begin to matter. They want to belong to clubs, play games, and enjoy childhood rituals (like avoiding stepping on cracks in the sidewalk). They want to please and be good, will endure the consequences of their actions, and take responsibility. Their attention span is longer—some may be able to work on a project for weeks. They have the beginnings of empathy, can see another's point of view, and discriminate somewhat between good and bad.

SPIRITUAL DEVELOPMENT

This is the "age of reason." Children are beginning to think for themselves. They want to know "why" and "how" and explore options. It's important to explain things to them in preparation for the next stage, when they will start making their own decisions. If you don't know the answers to their questions, search for them together. Teach them how to find answers and show them that you can always learn and grow. Don't simply say, "I don't know" or "Because I said so." At this stage children need the foundations of their faith solidly grounded.

These children need to be taken seriously as intellectual beings. This is a great time to teach them the underlying reasons for how they can know the Bible is God's book, how it's the manual for life from life's Manufacturer, how they can be sure Jesus is God, how you know God cares, and so on. They need to know that their faith is both *reasonable* (there are good reasons behind it) and *real* (it works in their lives). Teach them these things now to ensure that, when they hit their preteens and teens, they'll make choices based on what they know, rationally and experientially, to be true.

> When you show your children that what they believe is reasonable, their faith is given a solid anchor.

Children also need relational reasons for their faith. That is, they need to experience the results of actively trusting their loving God. They don't always connect an answer to prayer with a specific prayer they prayed earlier. You can play an important role by keeping track of these, showing them that their faith is real and practical. When they pray to find friends or for help on a test, show them the answers when they come. When they choose to tell the truth or not to steal, show them how it worked out because God's way works best. When they see concrete evidence of God's care, their beliefs about life become firmly established. They'll get into the habit of doing things God's way and going to God for help—because they'll know from experience that it works! They will have a growing collection of snapshots of God's faithfulness and the reliability of His principles.

When you show your children that what they believe is reasonable, their faith is given a solid anchor. When they experience God's love, their faith is real and practical.

KEY WAYS TO PREPARE THEIR MINDS

In the last stage, most of your children's "snapshots" had to do with people, relationships, and their expanding social world, with you always there in the background. As their lives expand, so do the experiences and memorable moments that form the basis of their lives and fill their albums. So now their pictures tend to focus on objects, experiences, and all manner of things they're curious about. And there, somewhere at the edge of the pictures, you can still be seen—your hand, eye, shoulder, or smile, visible and supportive. Here are a few things to consider as your children grow:

Continue to let your children in on the parenting process. Tell them that your job is to prepare them to do things themselves: have their own quiet times with God, read and study the Bible, choose God's way when no one is watching or there's pressure to do the opposite. Your job is to continue encouraging and loving them, but also to insist that they do their part. Their job is still to learn and take the next step. You'll be there to show them how and to make sure they understand where they're going. And God is always nearby.

Encourage and try to answer your children. Their questions will cover a lot of areas:

- Why certain behaviors are important, right or wrong
- Why God answers some prayers and not others
- Who God is and what He's like
- Why people do bad things
- Why some of their friends aren't Christians
- Why some who are Christians don't always act like it
- Why church is important
- Why God doesn't just do stuff without them praying
- Why Jesus had to die

These foundational truths are best taught in the context of making their faith real and reasonable, with an emphasis on God's love and care.

Show them examples from the Bible that address their concerns. Children at this age need to know that they can trust the Bible and God. When they understand these things, in the next stage they'll be ready to hang on and trust because they know God is in control and is working things out for their good. They'll start to understand that Bible stories are more than just stories—these stories help them know how to live. By the end of this stage, when they are grounded and growing, they will be able to tell their friends about who Jesus is, why Christianity works, what happened to them, and why they know it's real.

> Your children will begin to yield to God and put themselves in His hands. They'll begin developing their own relationship with God.

Prepare your children for what's coming. Each child develops differently and is ready to do more on his or her own—at his or her own pace. Match your approach to your children's needs and readiness. Be prepared for them to have very different concerns, speeds of learning, degrees of willingness to step out alone, and desire for your support. Whenever they move toward more autonomy, they're in transition to the next stage. Prepare them for what's coming in the various areas and give them a date, such as a specific birthday. Make the change something to look forward to.

For example, if you're planning to change your evening prayer times, tell them, "On your seventh (or eighth) birthday, you're going to start praying on your own—with us still helping and listening." On that day, if they're not ready, try alternate ways. You might say the prayers and have them repeat them after you. The next day, come up with their prayer list together and then have them say their prayers. You could alternate until they're ready to do it almost on their own. Be patient and go at their pace, but be insistent that they keep moving toward the next stage. Growth takes place one step at a time, not overnight.

Near the end of this stage your children will begin to yield to God and put themselves in His hands. They'll begin developing their own relationship with God. You will still do most of it with them, but toward the end of this stage they may want to start doing some of it on their own. Let them choose what time of day to do it—they might prefer after school or in the morning. The structure needs to work for them. This helps them move toward taking ownership in their relationship with God.

COMMON REFLECTIONS OF FAITH AT THIS AGE

As your children approach age 10, they need to be equipped with reasonable answers (geared to their level of understanding), a reasonable faith that they know is true, and the rationale behind the way they view the world. They'll be able to say, "I believe this. I'm going to build my life on God's way." They'll be ready to face the questions their expanding world will confront them with. They'll be moving toward reading their Bibles and going to church because they want to, and toward enjoying their times with God. They will get all the input you can possibly give them and know where to go for more (Sunday school, the pastor, other Christian leaders and adults, the Bible).

A lot of exploration of their faith is going on, and your children are beginning to find ways to express their own personal relationship with God. It's important to formalize this by creating another spiritual-life memory marker (like the day they were dedicated as babies and the day they first accepted Jesus as Savior and Lord). Near the end of this stage, you could set aside a specific time with each of your children. Make it significant in some way—a special meal out or a dedicated evening just for them. During your time together, affirm their faith and remember, out loud, their earlier memory markers. Give them any additional explanations about salvation they may need. Now that they can understand it more fully, they may have questions. Reaffirm their commitments to follow and obey God. Remind them of answered prayers they've experienced and emphasize that their faith is true and God is real. Ask them about their experiences with God and some of the events that have helped them truly know God is with them. Tell them your own faith story.

You may mark this occasion by preparing gifts for them. Give them a certificate (or framed Bible verse or special quote) with the date and a couple of sentences of explanation or a significant answered prayer. Let them choose the frame so it can become part of their decor and life. Then give them a "Faith Stories Journal" to track their relationship with God. This is a notebook or blank book set aside specifically to write down their experiences with God and prayer. You can start it by entering the dates of their infant dedication and their prayer for salvation and the date of your special evening out. You might also get them started by recording some of the answers to prayer you've seen in their lives, and perhaps a dedication. Encourage them to take over and record in it the things God does for them; what they learn as they continue to grow in their relationship with Him; prayers and their answers; how God blesses them; things they want God's help to understand; and so on.

When they make these records of their spiritual lives, they will be able to look back and see God's faithfulness alongside their own growth.

THINGS ABOUT GOD THEY'RE READY TO LEARN

This chart shows the information your children are ready to learn. In each area, topics they can grasp are listed. Along with giving them an

Ages 7–9

KNOWING		LOVING	LIVING	
A. Who God Is	B. What God Has Done	C. You Can Have a Relationship with God	D. You Can Be All God Wants You to Be	E. You Can Do All God Wants You to Do
1. You can be sure that God is real.	8. The Bible is true. It is God's Word, and you can trust it.	16. You read the Bible to learn about who God is (Father, Son, and Holy Spirit) and what He has done and is doing.	23. God wants you to learn and grow and become like Jesus.	29. Church is God's idea. Jesus is the head of the church. At church you learn about God and encourage each other to follow Jesus.
2. There is only one God.	9. God made sure all stories in the Bible together tell the One Big Story.	17. You can pray your own prayers with your parents.	24. Growth is a learning process.	30. God wants you to understand what a blessing people and good relationships are.
3. God exists in three Persons: Father, Son, and Holy Spirit. This is called the "Trinity."	10. The Bible you have is exactly what God wanted to give you.	18. Prayer benefits you in many ways.	25. Your character should match God's character.	31. God has taught you right from wrong. He did this to keep you safe and to give you a good life.
4. God (Father, Son, and Holy Spirit) is eternal.	11. God wants you to learn and study the Bible.	19. Keep praying: Persistence, tests, and trials.	26. God wants you to develop your talents.	32. The Ten Commandments are good guidelines for life.
5. Jesus is both God and Man.	12. The world is full of sin. There is an enemy in the world (Satan). Not everyone obeys God.	20. You can trust God and turn your life over to Him.	27. God wants you to develop the Fruit of the Spirit.	33. God wants you to share your faith.
6. Nothing exists apart from God.	13. Jesus died to save you from the penalty for sin.	21. You should learn to seek God.	28. God wants you to mature and develop your personality.	
7. God's character is true, honest, loving, compassionate, generous, selfless, forgiving, merciful, trustworthy, faithful, just, impartial, and holy.	14. Jesus defeated sin and Satan.	22. Jesus gives you peace.		
	15. Jesus is the only way to God.			

understanding of the "whys" and "hows," make an effort to always bring the topic back to the practical: How does this affect their lives? What does this mean to them where they are now? Isn't it amazing how much they'll learn in these exciting years of their childhood?

CHAPTER 10

- - - - - - - - - -

Knowing

The Deeper Reality of God's Character and Actions

These foundational years are exciting ones, as truths your children have been learning from the cradle suddenly take on new reality. Your children will want to grapple with truths you've touched on many times, now using their own powers of reasoning and their own volition to make them their own. Here are some of the truths about who God is and what He has done.

LEARNING MORE ABOUT WHO GOD IS

YOU CAN BE SURE GOD IS REAL.

How do you know God is real? Children in this stage often want to know. The apostle Paul pointed out that the world God created makes it obvious He exists: "What may be known about God is plain to them, because God has made it plain to them. For since the creation of the world God's invisible qualities—his eternal power and divine nature—have been clearly seen, being understood from what has been made, so that men are without excuse" (Romans 1:19-20). You can help your children understand that our beautiful, incredibly complicated, amazingly intertwined universe clearly shows the hand of a Creator.

Start with the assumption that your children already think God is real. Build on their belief. When they ask questions, assume they ask out of curiosity and a desire to know rather than out of skepticism. They want to have their faith bolstered. Make these truths a matter-of-fact, comforting addition to their faith.

> How do you know God is real? Children in this stage often want to know.

Give your children good reasons to believe. Share with them the following aspects of creation, including some things found in ourselves, that show God's hand:

Orderliness. Things fall down, never up. Water boils when you add heat. Wood burns. Every day the sun rises and sets. The world is so predictable and orderly that scientists can make rules about it. This could not happen by chance. It makes sense to believe that God designed it all!

Beauty. From newborns to nasturtiums, the world is full of beauty. Why? There's no reason for beauty except to give pleasure. Why would something with no function "evolve"? Only God would make something purely for enjoyment.

The God Idea. As long as there have been people, they have believed in God or gods. Where did that idea come from? God put it into people. He made humans to know that He's real. Even people who say they don't believe in God often turn to Him in trouble. We're made to need something or Someone other than ourselves—God.

Right and Wrong. Listen to people argue and you'll hear, "But you promised!" "It's not fair." People think that promises should be kept and that fairness is important. How does everyone know this? Because there's a law or rule built into everyone that says so. Your conscience tells you when you break this "rule." Where did this law come from? From God, who made right and wrong and who made people.

THERE IS ONLY ONE GOD.

Hearing that there's only one God can be welcome news to children. It gives them the security of knowing that the "rules" won't change and the hope that they can relate directly to Him. Take your children right into the promises of Scripture on this point, such as: "I am he. Before me no god was formed, nor will there be one after me" (Isaiah 43:10) and "I am the first and I am the last; apart from me there is no God" (Isaiah 44:6).

GOD EXISTS IN THREE PERSONS: FATHER, SON, AND HOLY SPIRIT.

This three-aspect wholeness is called the "Trinity" or "Three in One." God is a whole—One. That means you can't divide Him into parts. At the same time, He is three Persons. Jesus' baptism gives a clear picture of this: Jesus was in the water, the Father spoke from heaven, and the Spirit came down like a dove (Matthew 3:16-17).

You can help your children differentiate between the three Persons of God by pointing out their differing jobs: The Father is the source of everything. He sent His Son (see John 5:37; 1 Corinthians 8:6). The Son, Jesus, when He was on earth, showed who God is and what He's like. He's your role model and example. He died to save you from your sins. He will judge everyone in the end (see John 5:22; Romans 5:8; 8:33-34; Hebrews 10:30). The Holy Spirit helps you get to know God and grow as His child. He guides you into the life God has planned for you. He's with you, teaches you, and gives you gifts to help you do what God wants (see John 14:16-17, 26; 1 Corinthians 12:4; 2 Thessalonians 2:13).

GOD (FATHER, SON, AND HOLY SPIRIT) IS ETERNAL.

God created time along with everything else, so it can't have any effect on Him. What does that mean? God is never rushed! Your children never need to worry about Him running out of time—or disappearing. He is always around—always was, always will be.

There will be no end to God: "[The heavens] will perish, but you remain" (Hebrews 1:11).

Alpha and omega are the first and last letters of the Greek alphabet. This Scripture refers to the fact that God has no beginning and no end: " 'I am the Alpha and the Omega,' says the Lord God, 'who is, and who was, and who is to come, the Almighty' " (Revelation 1:8).

JESUS IS BOTH GOD AND MAN.

Jesus is God—and human, too: "[Jesus], being in very nature God, did not consider equality with God something to be grasped, but made himself nothing, taking the very nature of a servant, being made in human likeness" (Philippians 2:6-7). He lived on earth, showing people what God the Father is like. It's a mystery how someone can be divine and human, but with God everything is possible. Because Jesus is God, He could live perfectly and pay for our sins; because He is human, He knows from experience what it's like to walk in your children's shoes.

NOTHING EXISTS APART FROM GOD.

Not only did God make everything; He keeps it going: "For in him we live and move and have our being" (Acts 17:28). God is the ultimate source of everything: "God, for whom and through whom everything exists" (Hebrews 2:10).

Point out to your children that God's qualities all fit together. For example, if God is the only God but not eternal, then something could exist when He's not around—possibly other gods. Or if God did not know everything, how could He do everything? There would be things He wouldn't know how to do! God is either all of these things or none of them.

Pray that your children will want to know God and what He's like. Fuel their desire to discover more about Him by admitting that you don't know all there is to know about Him and that you're learning more all the time.

GOD IS AWESOME

"Who has measured the waters in the hollow of his hand . . . ? Who has held the dust of the earth in a basket, or weighed the mountains on the scales and the hills in a balance? Who has understood the mind of the LORD, or instructed him as his counselor? Whom did the LORD consult to enlighten him, and who taught him the right way? . . .

" 'To whom will you compare me? Or who is my equal?' " says the Holy One. . . .

"Do you not know? Have you not heard? The LORD is the everlasting God, the Creator of the ends of the earth. He will not grow tired or weary, and his understanding no one can fathom. He gives strength to the weary and increases the power of the weak." Isaiah 40:12-14, 25, 28-29

Sometimes we try to put God in a box—to make Him small, safe, and completely understandable. But we need to take all the limits off God; there are none! You can get this point across to your children by having them go through your home and collect a variety of boxes—shoeboxes, large cartons, lunch boxes, tiny jewelry boxes. Put all the boxes on the floor and ask, "Which of these boxes would God fit into? Do you think He'd like to live in a box? Why might somebody try to keep Him in a box?" Explain that even though God wants to be our friend, we can't "tame" Him, turn Him into a "pet," or control Him. He's always bigger and more powerful than our words can describe. We can expect life with Him to be full of surprises, to blow us away!

GOD'S CHARACTER IS . . .

Here are seven of God's character qualities that your children can begin to grasp at this stage.

1. *God is true and honest.* When God makes a promise, He fulfills it. You can count on Him to do what He says and be who He says. His Son, Jesus, showed us how to live a completely honest life. He is the God of truth: "Into your hands I commit my spirit; redeem me, O LORD, the God of truth" (Psalm 31:5).
2. *God is loving and compassionate.* God does not just feel loving or do

loving things; He is love: "God is love" (1 John 4:8). This can give your children great confidence in approaching and trusting Him.

3. *God is generous and selfless.* God gives good gifts, even when He doesn't have to: " 'See if I will not throw open the floodgates of heaven and pour out so much blessing that you will not have room enough for it' " (Malachi 3:10). He loved us even when we didn't love back.

4. *God is forgiving and merciful.* Thankfully, God doesn't give us what we deserve: "The LORD our God is merciful and forgiving, even

though we have rebelled against him" (Daniel 9:9). He forgives. While He lived on earth, Jesus forgave sins and mercifully healed people.

5. *God is trustworthy and faithful.* Your children can put their lives in God's hands, knowing that He will take care of them and guide them: "Know therefore that the LORD your God is God;

he is the faithful God, keeping his covenant of love to a thousand generations of those who love him and keep his commands" (Deuteronomy 7:9). He never goes back on His word or plays tricks on us.

6. *God is just and impartial.* God can't be bribed or manipulated: "He is the Rock, his works are perfect, and all his ways are just" (Deuteronomy 32:4). He'll always be as loving and involved in your children's lives as in anyone else's.

7. *God is holy.* There's nothing wrong, impure, dirty, sly, or under-handed in God. He's perfect. His Son, Jesus, lived a sinless life, showing people what holy living is: "You are to be holy to me because I, the LORD, am holy" (Leviticus 20:26).

To help children remember God's character traits, encourage them to come up with a visual symbol for each one; for example, a judge's gavel for justice and impartiality, and a bar of soap for holiness (purity). Have them draw these on a poster. Or use them in a guessing game, to see whether family members can figure out what the symbols represent.

As you teach your children what God is like, help them to see small ways in which they can develop some of the same character traits. For instance, a child might reflect God's generosity by letting a sibling read a favorite magazine first when it comes in the mail. Encourage children to commit to a specific action to be carried out on a specific day.

LEARNING MORE ABOUT WHAT GOD HAS DONE

THE BIBLE IS TRUE. IT IS GOD'S WORD, AND YOU CAN TRUST IT.

Your children may ask how you know the Bible is true and trustworthy. What will you tell them? The simple answer is that it can be trusted because it's God's book. You can know it's God's book because of how it came to be.

"All Scripture is God-breathed" (2 Timothy 3:16). The inspiration came to the prophets and other writers by the Holy Spirit: "Above all, you must understand that no prophecy of Scripture came about by the prophet's own interpretation. For prophecy never had its origin in the will of man, but men spoke from God as they were carried along by the Holy Spirit" (2 Peter 1:20-21).

As you approach this topic, assume that your children believe the Bible is God's Word. Offering evidence simply preempts doubts and prepares them for the next stage.

Want evidence to back up your claim that the Bible is God's book? Tell your children about where it came from and what scholars have discovered about the Bible.

God used more than 40 people to help Him write the Bible's 66 books. He used their personalities, ways of speaking, cultures, and experiences to write down exactly what He wanted us to have. Some of the people God used were rich; others were poor. They were

> As you teach your children what God is like, help them to see small ways in which they can develop some of the same character traits.

kings, poets, prophets, generals, priests, farmers, shepherds, fishermen, prisoners—even a doctor and a politician. They lived over a period of 1,500 years, on three continents, and spoke different languages. Yet they all agreed about life, God, and right and wrong! Without God overseeing this process it would have been impossible.

Over the years, many have doubted the Bible. Since they had no other sources that talked about some of the things in the Bible, they said the Bible was wrong. Then archaeologists began studying old things to learn about the past. They found evidence that confirmed what the Bible said. For example: People thought that Pontius Pilate wasn't a real person. If he was, he wouldn't have been called "Prefect," as the New Testament calls him. However, archaeologists found a large stone in Caesarea saying "Pontius Pilate, Prefect of Judea."

If your children show interest in this area, you might find some of the following resources helpful: *The New Evidence That Demands a Verdict* by Josh McDowell and *801 Questions Kids Ask about God* by Dave Veerman et al.

GOD MADE SURE ALL STORIES IN THE BIBLE TOGETHER TELL THE ONE BIG STORY.

It's important to know how Bible stories fit together. Without this, your children will have difficulty keeping Bible events and characters straight or understanding how Scripture as a whole points to Christ. If you haven't already read them "God's One Big Story" summarizing the Bible (see the appendix to this book on page 177), this would be a good time to do so.

Help your children understand how the Old and New Testaments fit together to express the One Big Story: "In the past God spoke to our forefathers through the prophets at many times and in various ways, but in these last days he has spoken to us by his Son, whom he appointed heir of all things, and through whom he made the universe" (Hebrews 1:1-2).

Help children learn the order of Bible events with the following

game. Write at least 10 of the major events (Creation, the Flood, David's reign, Jesus' birth, Paul's ministry, etc.) on index cards, mix them up, and have kids line them up in the proper order. When children have learned the order of the biggest events, do the same with other events (high points of Jesus' ministry, for example) and characters.

Try a "sword drill" using a children's Bible or Bible storybook. Call out the name of a story ("Moses and the Burning Bush," for instance) and see whether your children can find it. Do this with several stories, helping as needed. After playing the game several times, children will have improved their grasp of how the stories fit into the Bible's chronology.

THE BIBLE YOU HAVE IS EXACTLY WHAT GOD WANTED TO GIVE YOU.

God has guarded the Bible over the centuries so that what Christians have is what He wants them to have. For many hundreds of years before the first printing press, Scripture was copied by hand—carefully. We can be sure it is God's Word to us: "We did not follow cleverly invented stories when we told you about the power and coming of our Lord Jesus Christ, but we were eyewitnesses of his majesty" (2 Peter 1:16).

If your children want evidence for the Bible's accuracy, talk with them about where Bible manuscripts came from and how they were preserved. The older the copy we have of something is, the more accurate it probably is—since it was copied from things that were closer to the original and so there were fewer chances for mistakes to be made. There are over 5,000 old, handwritten copies or parts of copies of the New Testament. The oldest is part of the Gospel of John, copied only 20 to 70 years after John wrote it. Imagine, if John had children or grandchildren, they could have seen or touched it! There are also tens of thousands of pieces of copies of the Old Testament. And scholars have the whole New Testament from only 300 years after the last book in it was written!

Comparing these manuscripts to today's Bibles shows that it hasn't changed in any way that affects what we believe.

When manuscripts from different places and times say the same things, it shows they were copied accurately. Until 1947, the oldest piece of the Old Testament was from 800 years after Jesus. But the Dead Sea Scrolls were discovered that year; they included a copy of Isaiah from about 200 years before Jesus—a thousand years older than the oldest copy we had—and the two are almost exactly the same!

The stories about Jesus, the Gospels, were written down less than 50 years after the events happened. Many people who had been there at the time, or their children (who had probably heard the stories umpteen times), would still have been alive. If the stories were wrong, they would have said so.

To bring home how amazing the Bible's accuracy is, get your children to copy several verses by hand. They're bound to make a mistake or two—and that's only in one small section. Talk about how amazingly accurate our Scripture manuscripts are!

GOD WANTS YOU TO LEARN AND STUDY THE BIBLE.

When it comes to maps, the Bible is the most valuable one you can find—if you want to arrive at the goal of a fulfilling life that serves God.

Help your children learn to refer to it for direction.

Children won't study the Bible unless they know it's the authority for all of life's decisions. Reinforce that truth by letting your children see you go to God's Word for answers. Help them to capture the psalmist's love for God's words: "Oh, how I love your law! I meditate on it all day long. Your commands make me wiser than my enemies, for they are ever with me. I have more insight than all my teachers, for I meditate on your statutes. I have more understanding than the elders, for I obey your precepts. . . . I gain understanding from your precepts; therefore I hate every wrong path. Your word is a lamp to my feet and a light for my path" (Psalm 119:97-100, 104-105).

Give them the reason for diligent study: God's Word points to all the truth about Jesus and tells us everything we need to believe in Him. "These are written that you may believe that Jesus is the Christ, the Son of God, and that by believing you may have life in his name" (John 20:31).

When your children face challenges—a test, surgery, the death of a grandparent—go to the Bible with them to find its advice on the subject. Make a habit of asking, "What does the Bible say about this?" Discuss what you find. Show older children in this age group how to locate relevant passages in a concordance. Some Bibles also list verses to read when facing specific struggles—everything from money problems to grief. Call children's attention to helps like these.

Keep at least one easy-to-read Bible accessible, especially in a well-traveled area, so children can see it's ready to use as life's instruction manual.

Help children begin to see the difference between reading and studying the Bible. Explain that we read to help us grow in our relationship with God; after all, spending time with His book is spending time with Him. Studying the Bible is about finding out what to do in specific situations and learning to do things God's way. It's like mining for gold.

THE WORLD IS FULL OF SIN. THERE IS AN ENEMY IN THE WORLD. NOT EVERYONE OBEYS GOD.

Evil can be an uncomfortable subject. But your children are growing up in a world that's disfigured by the results of sin, and they need to know why. They need to know that Satan is real, that he has power on earth—and that Jesus has ultimately defeated him. They need to know that bad things happen because of sin's side effects, and that Satan has blinded many people to the truth of God's Word.

Explain to your children where Satan came from (heaven, an angel): "How you have fallen from heaven, O morning star, son of the dawn!

You have been cast down to the earth. . . . You said in your heart, 'I will ascend to heaven . . . I will make myself like the Most High.' But you are brought down to the grave, to the depths of the pit" (Isaiah 14:12-15). A long time ago, an angel named Lucifer ("morning star") rebelled against God. He wanted all the power—to be like God and to replace God. His sin led to his being thrown out of heaven and sent to earth. Other angels—now demons—chose to follow him. On earth he told the first lie and tricked Adam and Eve into disobeying God too. That was just the beginning.

Satan is powerful. But he was created—so he's far, far less powerful than God. He can't create. The Bible calls him a liar and the father of lies because he started out with lying and he's still at it. He hates God and anyone who follows God, so he tries to keep people away from God. He loves evil.

But you and your children don't need to be afraid. When Jesus died and rose again, Satan's power was broken. For help against him, all a Christian has to do is go to God and ask. Satan hates that!

Your children should know that they don't need to fear Satan because they belong to God: "Submit yourselves, then, to God. Resist the devil, and he will flee from you. Come near to God and he will come near to you" (James 4:7-8).

Give your child the future expectation of a day when Christ will ultimately banish Satan from the earth: "The creation waits in eager expectation for the sons of God to be revealed. For the creation was subjected to frustration, not by its own choice, but by the will of the one who subjected it, in hope that the creation itself will be liberated from its bondage to decay and brought into the glorious freedom of the children of God. We know that the whole creation has been groaning as in the pains of childbirth right up to the present time" (Romans 8:19-22).

Why do bad things happen? Satan is part of the reason bad things happen in the world. But people do bad things, too, when they decide their way is better than God's. And every time it leads to trouble!

God wants people to be free to choose to love Him. So He gave everyone a free will—the ability to make choices. Because people are sinful, they often choose wrong things. Every wrong choice has consequences. Some bad things happen because people make evil or bad choices. God could stop it, but that would mean taking away people's free will. He lets people have what they choose, but He can turn the bad into good to help us grow.

Other bad things, like death and disease, are a result of sin too. This doesn't mean that people who get sick are being punished for their sins. It means that when Adam and Eve sinned, it affected every created thing. Because we live in a world where Satan still has power, there is pain and suffering. But the end of the story is clear: Jesus wins!

Your children will meet people who don't believe in God, who believe wrong things about Him, or who follow different religions. Your children can understand that the reason many people reject the truth about Jesus is that Satan is hard at work: "The god of this age has blinded the minds of unbelievers, so that they cannot see the light of the gospel of the glory of Christ, who is the image of God" (2 Corinthians 4:4).

Some people don't want to believe in God. Some have seen "Christians" who didn't act like followers of Jesus. They think, *If that's what believing in God does to you, I don't want it.* Others don't want to believe because they don't like being told what they can or can't do. They like sinning and don't want to hear that what they're doing is wrong. Still others simply don't know about Jesus. Or their families have taught them to believe in other religions. We can pray for them—and let them know why we believe as we do.

When you're talking about the devil and his demons, keep the focus on God. Emphasize that God is in control and has His plan on track. Yes, there's a roaring lion wanting your children to do wrong and to destroy their lives, but Jesus overcame the devil. Your children can overcome too. If they're afraid of Satan or demons, remind them that Jesus is with them all the time—and He's much stronger than Satan. All they have to do is pray for help. Jesus will keep them safe as they follow Him.

JESUS DIED TO SAVE YOU FROM THE PENALTY FOR SIN. JESUS DEFEATED SIN AND SATAN. JESUS IS THE ONLY WAY TO GOD.

If your children don't yet know why and how to accept Jesus as their Savior, you can tell them. Focus the explanation around their need for salvation because they have sinned, and God's provision of a Savior, Jesus: "For all have sinned and fall short of the glory of God, and are justified freely by his grace through the redemption that came by Christ Jesus. God presented him as a sacrifice of atonement, through faith in his blood. He did this to demonstrate his justice, because in his forbearance he had left the sins committed beforehand unpunished—he did it to demonstrate his justice at the present time, so as to be just and the one who justifies those who have faith in Jesus" (Romans 3:23-26).

As one child in this stage asked, "Why did Jesus have to die? It isn't fair." Younger children may simply accept without questioning that Jesus died for them. In this stage, questions are more likely. If your children wonder why the sacrifice of Jesus was necessary, explain to them that Jesus didn't have to die—He chose to, out of love. God loves the world. He wants to have with everyone the kind of close relationship He had with Adam and Eve in the very beginning. The only way to do that was to take care of the sin problem.

God made people and chose to be their Father. He chose to be responsible for them. Think of it this way: In a store, parents pay for what their children break. If parents don't pay, who will? The child usually can't. In a similar way, God made Himself responsible to pay for the thing His children "broke"—their relationship with Him. He did this knowing what it would cost, because He was a loving Father. If He didn't pay for it, who could? No one.

The punishment for sin is death. Since everyone sins, everyone would have to pay the death penalty. Only someone who was not born sinful (which excludes everyone since Adam and Eve) could die for others. Everyone else could die only for himself or herself. The only perfect person is Jesus. He defeated Satan and sin when He died and rose again. This is why Jesus is the only way to God.

CHAPTER 11

■ ■ ■ ■ ■ ■ ■ ■

Loving

Your 7–9-Year-Old's Deepening Relationship with God

Maybe your child prayed to receive Christ's gift of salvation as a pre-schooler or kindergartner. Maybe these growing years of seven to nine will mark that special turning point. Either way, these years are ones when children grow in all their relationships—especially in friendship with God. These points of learning are the ones that most strongly affect a child's direct relationship with the Creator.

DEVELOPING A FRIENDSHIP WITH GOD

YOU READ THE BIBLE TO LEARN ABOUT WHO GOD IS (FATHER, SON, AND HOLY SPIRIT) AND WHAT HE HAS DONE AND IS DOING.

As they move through this stage, your children may want more and more to know why it's so important to read the Bible. Their questions usually will flow from curiosity, not doubt, as they look for information to back up their faith and for a reason to keep reading the Bible.

Let them know that the Bible is a living book. The Holy Spirit uses it to teach them to deal with whatever they're facing. It applies to their lives:

"These are the commands, decrees and laws the LORD your God directed me to teach you to observe in the land that you are crossing the Jordan to possess, so that you, your children and their children after them may fear the LORD your God as long as you live by keeping all his decrees and commands that I give you, and so that you may enjoy long life" (Deuteronomy 6:1-2).

Your children's personal Bible storybook needs to grow with them. As their ability to read increases, they'll need a new book that contains more of the Bible stories and tells them in more detail. They'll begin to want to read some of a story on their own and some with you. Encourage them to read stories to you, too.

Continue to reinforce the idea of a regular time in the Bible. Pray with your children before reading Scripture; help them expect God to teach them from it. Expect this for yourself, too. If you're learning from Bible stories alongside your children, they'll see this as "the way it is" and look forward to it.

> Let your children know that the Bible is a living book. The Holy Spirit uses it to teach them to deal with whatever they're facing.

Encourage personal Bible reading time by placing a children's Bible, Bible storybook, or children's devotional book next to your child's bed. Some children at this stage find it comforting to read Bible stories or other faith-oriented books at bedtime, especially if they struggle with fears of the dark or bad dreams.

Toward the end of this stage, most children will be able to begin reading their Bible storybook and talking to God on their own. Encourage them to pick up their Bible storybook and read it even when you're not there. God can speak to them through it. They're ready to begin to see that their relationship with God is their very own—and they can experience it with no one else around.

Their time in God's Word "hides" God's truths in their hearts—a treasure and training for all the days of their lives: "I seek you with all my heart; do not let me stray from your commands. I have hidden your word in my heart that I might not sin against you" (Psalm 119:10-11).

YOU CAN PRAY YOUR OWN PRAYERS WITH YOUR PARENTS.

It's time to take prayer to the next level! Your children may still pray with you, but most of the prayers are now theirs. Step back and let them take more initiative. Encourage them to pray conversational prayers anytime during the day, as well as "business" prayers at set times that cover more fully the topics God wants us to talk to Him about: "In the same way, the Spirit helps us in our weakness. We do not know what we ought to pray for, but the Spirit himself intercedes for us with groans that words cannot express. And he who searches our hearts knows the mind of the Spirit, because the Spirit intercedes for the saints in accordance with God's will" (Romans 8:26-27).

"What should I pray about?" Whether or not children ask this question, they often need help thinking of topics to bring before their heavenly Father. You can lift them out of the "God bless everybody" rut by pointing them to the types of praying found in the Lord's Prayer (see Matthew 6:9-13 and Luke 11:2-4). Here are a few specific types:

1. *Thank-you prayers.* Show appreciation for who God is and what He's done.

2. P*rayers about God's kingdom.* Pray that you—and everyone, everywhere—will do what God wants. Ask that other people will come to know Jesus and that Jesus' church will grow strong so it can do its job.

3. *Leader prayers.* Pray that leaders and those in authority (even teachers and baby-sitters) will obey God.

4. *Personal requests.* Pray about your own needs and concerns—for health, protection, friendship, etc.
5. *Growing prayers.* Confess wrongs and ask for forgiveness; pray about becoming a stronger Christian.
6. *Prayer for others.* Ask God to help friends, family, and anyone else with needs.
7. *Guidance prayers.* Pray for God to lead you, to help you make the best choices.
8. *Praise prayers.* "Cheer" for God because He's your Creator, and because He has the power to answer all your other prayers!

Sometimes children don't know how to express their fears, sadness, or even joy in their prayers. Assure them that God can help them know what to say. And because God understands what's in their hearts, He knows how they feel even if all they can do is sigh or cry.

As your children become more independent, you can still help them develop a prayer list—written or unwritten—by discussing the day's events and helping them choose concerns and blessings to pray about.

After prayer, instead of rushing straight to good-night kisses or some other activity, try having a short period of quiet. This reinforces the fact that God is there and that we need to listen in case He wants to give us wisdom on how to deal with an issue we've prayed about. Avoid implying that children should expect audible answers, but assure them that God responds in His way and time.

PRAYER BENEFITS YOU IN MANY WAYS.

Just as children ask why they should read the Bible, they'll ask why they should pray. The main benefit is a relationship with the Creator of the universe, who loves them very much. Out of this relationship, built by prayer, come several other benefits:

- Joy and peace (John 16:24; Philippians 4:6-7)
- Wisdom and understanding (Proverbs 2:3, 5-6; Jeremiah 33:3)

- Strength and courage (Psalm 138:3)
- Protection and rescue from harm and evil (Psalm 22:4)
- Purpose and guidance (Psalm 57:2)
- Meeting of our needs (Romans 8:32)
- Fulfillment of our desires (Psalm 37:4)
- Help and encouragement (Psalm 10:17)

Use comparisons to help your children understand prayer. For example, prayer is like a telephone (it keeps you in touch with your Friend—God); a map (it helps you find landmarks, danger spots, and the best way to get places); clothes (it protects you); a party (it's a time of thanksgiving and celebration with your best Friend); and a tree house (it's a private place for you to spend time with your good Friend and share your thoughts with no fear of them getting spread around).

Do your children wonder why they don't always get what they ask for in prayer? Try explaining it this way: "If you ask me at your age, 'Can I borrow the car?' you'll get an automatic no. If you ask, 'May I do my homework?' you'll probably get an automatic yes. If you ask, 'May I play with my friend?' the answer will depend on what's best at the time. Prayer is like that. Some prayers get an automatic no. For example, Saul (Paul) wanted God's help to persecute Jesus' followers. The answer was no. Prayers to get away with stealing or to help you get back at someone will get a no  because God won't help you do something wrong. Other prayers get an automatic yes. For example, a prayer for forgiveness, to understand the Bible, to become more like Jesus, to find a way to help someone else, for courage to tell someone about Jesus—all these get a yes. After all, God tells us to pray for these things! Then there are the less clear prayers, the ones the Bible isn't specific about. These might get a yes, a no, or a 'wait.' For example, you might pray, 'Help me make the team,' or 'Please give me a bike for my birthday,' or 'Please make Jenny want to be my friend.' The best thing to do when we pray about these things is to ask that God will work them out in the way that pleases Him most. That's what people mean when they pray for God's will. Then, whatever the answer is, you'll know it's what's best for you."

Sometimes God says no to a request because we're disobeying Him or fighting or not forgiving. He may put our request "on hold" until we deal with that issue. In any case, God hears every prayer, and He answers according to what's best for us.

KEEP PRAYING: PERSISTENCE, TESTS, AND TRIALS.

A best friend is moving away; a beloved pet is dying; a bully continues to rule the playground. Your children have prayed about these things, but God hasn't granted their requests. How can you help them deal with the disappointment?

Even at this age, your children's faith will be tested. Bring them back to the fact of God's love. God cares about their feelings, but He also knows what's best. He wants us to keep praying and not give up. Timing is in His hands.

So are the answers. We may not like or understand them. The hard truth is that God wants our faith to grow strong and to be focused on the right things—His love and care—and not on getting what we want or having a smooth life. It's not easy to help our children or ourselves move from "Why don't You . . . ?" to "I trust You, God, even if I don't understand." But you can begin this process together, starting with your example as you learn to accept what God sends and allows: "Not only so, but we also rejoice in our sufferings, because we know that suffering produces perseverance; perseverance, character; and character, hope. And hope does not disappoint us, because God has poured out his love into our hearts by the Holy Spirit, whom he has given us" (Romans 5:3-5).

Help your children see their troubles as "worth it" for the ultimate result: "These have come so that your faith—of greater worth than gold, which perishes even though refined by fire—may be proved genuine and may result in praise, glory and honor when Jesus Christ is revealed" (1 Peter 1:7).

Try the following one day at lunch or dinner. Bring out a pathetic-looking meal, perhaps a couple of crackers on a plate. Say, "I'm going to give you a choice. You can eat this now, or you can wait 20 minutes. If you wait, I have something better planned—but I won't tell you what it is." Let your kids decide whether to wait. For those who do, serve a favorite food 20 minutes later. Use this as an object lesson to reinforce the truth that sometimes God makes us wait because He has something far better planned.

As you learn to trust God during tests and trials, be honest with Him and with your children. Show them in the psalms how David swung back and forth between frustration and praise, reinforcing the truth that it's okay to express your real feelings to God. It's also important to come back to trusting Him, as David did.

Ask your children to list all the junk food they think they could eat in a single day. Then ask them whether eating all that stuff would really be a good idea. Explain that even though eating a lot of junk food might feel good, it would hurt them in the long run. In the same way, God knows that some of our requests might make us happy for a while but would end up hurting us. Assure your children that God cares about how they feel, but He knows the big picture, too.

YOU CAN TRUST GOD AND TURN YOUR LIFE OVER TO HIM.

Who knows the best way to use a computer, mountain bike, or video camera? The person who designed and made it! The designer can tell you how everything was meant to work, how to get the most out of that thing, and what not to do with it. As the Designer of life, God knows better than anyone else how life works. It only makes sense to abide by His guidelines: "Trust in the Lord with all your heart and lean not on your own understanding; in all your ways acknowledge him, and he will make your paths straight" (Proverbs 3:5-6).

For your children, turning their lives over to God means agreeing that

He knows what's best for them, and that He has a great plan for their lives. It means entrusting their dreams and ambitions to His care: "'If anyone would come after me, he must deny himself and take up his cross and follow me. For whoever wants to save his life will lose it, but whoever loses his life for me and for the gospel will save it'" (Mark 8:34-35).

> As the Designer of life, God knows better than anyone else how life works. It only makes sense to abide by His guidelines.

Facing a change in your family? Use your next time of uncertainty—looking for a new job, moving, or having financial difficulties—to teach your children what trust looks like. Gather your family together and entrust your situation to God, telling Him that you want His will even if it's different from yours.

If it's hard for you to trust God with your future, don't hide this fact from your children. Share your difficulty with them, though without going into more detail than is appropriate for your children. Be honest as you make an effort to grow in this area. They'll see that this "trusting God" stuff is practical, down-to-earth.

Say your eight-year-old son, Taylor, is new at school. He's trying to trust God to lead him to some new friends, but you don't see it happening. Should you step in? Before you do, consider that God may have something planned that you can't foresee and that Taylor may learn a valuable lesson by waiting and trusting. It's hard not to "answer" your children's prayers yourself when you see them becoming disappointed, and sometimes parents are meant to be God's vehicle to answer their children's prayers. But be careful not to rescue your children when you don't think God is answering. He may want to teach both of you something!

YOU SHOULD LEARN TO SEEK GOD.

The way to find God is to look for Him. This is one of the most important things you can teach your children. Seeking God isn't so much a matter of how much time your children spend praying and meditating on His Word (though it does take time); it's more a matter of wanting to follow God with all their hearts. The better they know God, the more they'll love Him and the more of Him they'll want: "As the deer pants for streams of water, so my soul pants for you, O God. My soul thirsts for God, for the living God. When can I go and meet with God?" (Psalm 42:1-2).

A serious, intentional choosing is what God wants from His children: "Seek first his kingdom and his righteousness, and all these things will be given to you as well" (Matthew 6:33). Do you seek God? Or do you feel more like you're running from Him? If the latter is the case, consider talking with your pastor, a Christian counselor, or an experienced Christian friend about the guilt, anger, or other feelings that may be keeping you from drawing closer to the Lord. If your children are to know what it looks like to seek God, it's best if they can see and hear you trying to know Him better.

Suggest ways in which your children can pray as they seek God. For example: "Dear God, please help me understand how You feel about me." Or "God, I'd really like to know why You seem angry in the Old Testament and loving in the New Testament." Don't make this something they must do. Rather, tell them that praying these prayers sincerely and regularly is a way to become closer to their heavenly Father.

JESUS GIVES YOU PEACE.

Why call Jesus the "Prince of Peace"? Because He can give us peace with God and peace in the middle of trying circumstances. Your children need to know they can go to Him when they're frustrated, confused, angry, or worried. Jesus is bigger than anything that upsets them; His peace can calm them in any situation: "You will keep in perfect peace him whose mind is steadfast, because he trusts in you" (Isaiah 26:3).

Children ages seven to nine are often much more aware of the dangers of the world they live in and often experience fears and "troubled hearts." Point them to the source of peace: "Peace I leave with you; my peace I give you. I do not give to you as the world gives. Do not let your hearts be troubled and do not be afraid" (John 14:27).

Point out to your children when they're lacking peace, so that they can begin to identify what its lack and its presence feel like. Examples: when your children panic because they forgot a page of homework; when they express doubt that they'll have enough money when they grow up; when they feel guilty over hitting a sibling; when they're angry over being treated unfairly by a teacher; when they're nervous about having to sing in a concert.

Conversely, make sure your children know what peace is. Tell them it's a quiet, settled, relaxed feeling. Point out peaceful times—a moment when family members are eating at the table without bickering, or a day when a child has made a confident speech in class. When they recognize its presence, they'll be able to ask God for peace more easily when it's absent.

Model going to God for peace when you need it. Does tension start you thinking about God's promises? Or do you find yourself heading for that half gallon of ice cream in the freezer? Let children see you taking time to calm down and to pray or read a Bible passage that offers comfort.

CHAPTER 12

——————

Living

How 7–9-Year-Olds Can Live Out Their Faith

In earlier chapters dealing with earlier stages of development, your children have learned that they live out their faith by *being* and *doing*—*being* God's family-member and *doing* what pleases God. In this stage of spiritual growth, these young believers will deepen their commitment to God's way.

BEING ALL GOD WANTS YOU TO BE

GOD WANTS YOU TO LEARN AND GROW AND BECOME LIKE JESUS.
Talk about role models! Jesus is the perfect example for your children. He showed by His life and teachings how God wants them to live: "I have set you an example that you should do as I have done for you" (John 13:15).

"Being like Jesus" could be confusing to your children. Explain that this doesn't mean wearing long robes, walking everywhere, and speaking in parables. They're to pattern themselves after Jesus' character.

For example, Jesus was compassionate: "When he saw the crowds, he had compassion on them, because they were harassed and helpless, like sheep without a shepherd" (Matthew 9:36).

And Jesus was a servant to others and directly instructed His followers also to be servants: "Jesus said to them, 'The kings of the Gentiles lord it over them; and those who exercise authority over them call themselves Benefactors. But you are not to be like that. Instead, the greatest among you should be like the youngest, and the one who rules like the one who serves. For who is greater, the one who is at the table or the one who serves? Is it not the one who is at the table? But I am among you as one who serves' " (Luke 22:25-27).

You can use other stories from the life of Jesus to show children how they need to be like Him. A great one is when *Jesus stands up to the devil*

(Matthew 4:1-11). Jesus refused to do things Satan's way. He trusted God to take care of Him and chose God's way. He quoted the Bible when He was in trouble.

Jesus was kind to an outcast leper (Mark 1:40-44). Most people avoided lepers. But Jesus touched this man and healed him. Jesus loved unpopular people and helped those whom others avoided.

Point out the way *Jesus tells it like it is* (Matthew 5:21-48; 11:20-24). Because He loved people, Jesus warned them when they were wrong. He was not afraid to call sin what it really is. He was straightforward and just.

Show your children how repeatedly *Jesus forgives rejection* (Luke 22:56-62; John 21:15-19). Jesus didn't hate Peter, who had denied Him. He forgave Peter and was his friend again. Jesus understood His friend and loved him no matter what.

Jesus had empathy for others' feelings (John 11:1-44). Jesus felt His friends' grief and cried with them. He let them see that He understood their pain.

Jesus serves others (John 13:1-17). He did the most lowly task—foot washing—for His friends. He served them willingly and selflessly.

What would Jesus do? Have children come up with real-life dilemmas they might encounter. For instance, at a friend's house the friend wants to watch a violent video your child knows is off-limits; at school, your child knows who stole trading cards from backpacks at recess. Ask, "What do you think Jesus would do in this situation? How do you know?" Point out that the answer to the question starts with who Jesus is as a Person—His character—and then is expressed in His actions.

GROWTH IS A LEARNING PROCESS.

Like physical growth, spiritual growth doesn't happen overnight. It occurs little by little as your children regularly spend time with God and internalize what they learn. It happens as they make right choices—and as they make mistakes and learn from them.

Your children need the comfort of knowing that growth involves mistakes and second tries. Instead of expecting instant perfection, God knows that becoming like Jesus is a process, just as is discovering how to write letters, memorizing multiplication tables, or painting pictures. This is why the Bible talks about "working out" your salvation: "Continue to work out your salvation with fear and trembling, for it is God who works in you to will and to act according to his good purpose" (Philippians 2:12-13).

Your children should understand that they have everything they need to grow spiritually: "His divine power has given us everything we need for life and godliness through our knowledge of him who called us by his own glory and goodness. . . . For this very reason, make every effort to add to your faith goodness; and to goodness, knowledge; and to knowledge, self-control; and to self-control, perseverance; and to perseverance, godliness; and to godliness, brotherly kindness; and to brotherly kindness, love. For if you

> Like physical growth, spiritual growth doesn't happen overnight. It occurs little by little as your children regularly spend time with God and internalize what they learn.

possess these qualities in increasing measure, they will keep you from being ineffective and unproductive in your knowledge of our Lord Jesus Christ" (2 Peter 1:3, 5-8).

Let your children know that you're growing too—as a person, a parent, and a follower of Jesus. Admit that you make mistakes and that you're learning from them. Treat mistakes—yours, theirs, and other people's—gently. Try to see errors as rungs on the ladder of growth rather than as failures.

Remember that appearances are not the most important thing. Focus on your children's hearts. Avoid pressuring them to act a certain way when their hearts are far from that; they must take ownership of the right attitude before their actions will mean anything. Pushing children's faith experience past their understanding and beyond their hearts can reduce their Christianity to a matter of performance—which implies that if they blow it, they're failures. Actions are important, but good actions mean the most when they flow from the heart.

Introduce "stretching" experiences in small steps. For example, instead of trying to teach your children to be good servants by making them sing solos at a nursing home, start by having them help you hand out birthday cards or treats at the facility. Work your way up to having the kids do more as they become comfortable in the unfamiliar environment. Give them small "success experiences" that build their confidence about doing the right thing. Embarrassing failures can cause children to fear trying again.

YOUR CHARACTER SHOULD MATCH GOD'S CHARACTER.

Does building godly character produce clones? Hardly! Character isn't the same as personality. Each child's personality is unique. Character, on the other hand, should be a reflection of who God is and what He's like: "The Son is the radiance of God's glory and the exact representation of his being" (Hebrews 1:3). It's the same for all people, but it's expressed in different ways through different personalities.

Why is character so important? Because good character will protect your children from evil. Doing things God's way builds a strong tower of protection around them.

— —

TEN GODLY QUALITIES (PSALM 15)

A godly person walks blamelessly, acts righteously, speaks truthfully, does his neighbor no wrong, casts no slur on others, despies the vile, honors those who fear God, keeps oaths even when it hurts, lends money without usury, and doesn't accept bribes.

— —

Here are seven key character traits of God that your children need to incorporate into their lives. A motto is included with each trait—a phrase with which children can affirm to themselves that they're growing in that area. Encourage kids to use the mottoes or come up with their own—and to make the phrases part of their identity by copying the words onto posters, jewelry, calendars, or other personal items they'll see frequently.

1. *Truth and honesty* (Ephesians 4:15): "God doesn't lie, and neither do I!"
2. *Love and compassion* (John 15:17; Colossians 3:12): "My heart's in the right place."
3. *Generosity and selflessness* (1 Timothy 6:18): "Something's got to give: me!"
4. *Forgiveness and mercy* (Colossians 3:13): "I forgive you."
5. *Trustworthiness and faithfulness* (Galatians 6:9-10): "Count on me!"
6. *Justice and impartiality* (Matthew 23:23): "Life's not fair, but I try to be."
7. *Holiness* (Romans 12:1): "Caution: Set apart."

Point out character traits at work in everyday life. For example, when your child's best friend decides to hang out with someone else, talk about faithfulness; when a child gets too much change at the store, talk about honesty.

Spell out the benefits of godly character. For instance, honesty works—it's as simple as that. A person who tells the truth consistently will be trusted; others will want him or her as a friend. In contrast, a dishonest person gets a bad reputation; others stop trusting that person with belongings, secrets, and responsibility. When your children understand the benefits of character, they'll be more likely to choose the right direction because they'll know it works best.

GOD WANTS YOU TO DEVELOP YOUR TALENTS.

Saxophone playing, somersaulting, storytelling, sewing—talents are God-given abilities: "Do you see a man skilled in his work? He will serve

before kings; he will not serve before obscure men" (Proverbs 22:29). Your children's talents are an important part of God's plan for them (see also Exodus 35:25-26, 30-35; 36:1; Proverbs 22:6; Daniel 1:17, 20).

Talents might come easy, but it takes work to develop them through music lessons, baseball practice, art classes, and so on. You can help your children reach the

potential God has in mind for them by identifying and cultivating their talents.

As your schedule and budget allow, encourage your children to try a variety of activities and lessons to help them discover their talents. Let them explore. When your children show an aptitude for something or enjoy a particular activity, affirm them in that and try to make it possible for them to grow in it.

Point out examples of people using their talents to serve God. Obvious ones might include those who sing songs about Jesus and those who preach, but don't overlook the rest—the photographer who stirs com-

passion by taking pictures of famine victims, the cook who prepares meals for visiting missionaries, the attorney who defends the poor, etc.

God needs people with talents—and willing hearts. Help your children make the most of their talents, but discourage them from bragging about their abilities or substituting talent for godly character. Encourage them to see how their abilities might be used to call people's attention to Jesus, not just to themselves.

GOD WANTS YOU TO DEVELOP THE FRUIT OF THE SPIRIT.

The fruit of the Spirit is so much more than just being nice. This group of qualities comes from inside, in your children's hearts, and can be developed only in cooperation with the Spirit of God. God's fruit makes relationships work and helps us to become more like Him. What are these fruit? "Love, joy, peace, patience, kindness, goodness, faithfulness, gentleness and self-control" (Galatians 5:22-23).

> Each child's personality is unique. Character, on the other hand, should be a reflection of who God is and what He's like.

Words like love, joy, and peace can sound admirable but vague. What does the fruit of the Spirit look like in real life? Here are some thoughts to help you prepare to teach your children about this subject.

1. *Love* is a commitment to unselfish thoughts, acts, and emotions. To give love, your children need to have their "love tanks" filled up by God's love—and yours. Love works by giving, listening, hugging, defending, and more. To help children "grow" love, remind them that other people are important because they're eternal and made in God's image, that God has made everyone different (and that's good), and that we need to think of others' concerns first (see Philippians 2:3-4; 1 John 4:16, 19).

2. *Joy* is a deep, cheerful contentment. It comes from understanding God's love and what Jesus did for us. It comes from accepting God's constant care and knowing that He'll never let us down. Joy

is contagious. Help children grow joy by reviewing their "thankful list," reminding them of how big God is, encouraging them to value each moment God gives them, and reminding them of heaven (see Romans 14:17; 1 Thessalonians 5:16; 1 Peter 1:8).

3. *Peace* is assurance that all is well because we serve a loving, wonderful God. Peaceful people tend to be relaxed, full of trust, confident. Peace with and from God becomes peace between them and others, too. Help your children grow peace by reminding them to focus on the fact that God is in charge, to tell God about every aspect of their lives, and to trust God to take care of all their concerns (see Isaiah 26:3; Ephesians 2:14).

4. *Patience* is showing God's grace to others despite what they "deserve." God is patient with us because He knows we're still growing. We need to remember that no one else is finished growing yet, either. Help your children grow patience by suggesting that they imagine everyone is wearing a button that says, "Please be patient; God isn't finished with me yet." When they're tempted to be impatient, kids can try "rewinding" and taking a deep breath until they can respond patiently (see Ephesians 4:2; Hebrews 12:3).

5. *Kindness* is being considerate of others' feelings. It includes being polite, going out of our way to encourage others, and never giving up on people. Children can grow kindness as they think about how others want to be treated, as they look for ways to help people, and as they watch their words (see Luke 6:35-36; Colossians 3:12).

6. *Goodness* is choosing right over wrong. God is completely good—always perfect, always right. Goodness isn't just a matter of not doing bad things; it's doing the right thing. Children can begin to grow goodness by listening to their consciences and to God's Spirit, and by learning from the Bible what God says is right (see Nahum 1:7; Galatians 6:10).

7. *Faithfulness* is a constant commitment to God and people, and a constant expression of that commitment. It's doing what we say we'll do, taking care of what we're responsible for, and obeying God

no matter how others act. The Holy Spirit may use difficult times to teach your children faithfulness. They also can grow faithfulness by remembering that God doesn't change no matter how people treat Him and by vowing to be the same way: "God never gives up, so neither do I!" (see Deuteronomy 7:9; Galatians 6:9).

8. *Gentleness* is an inner strength that lets us serve others without feeling threatened or inferior. It never hurts another person's feelings or dreams. It's a strong, selfless caring. You can help children grow gentleness by assuring them that they're loved; when they know that, they can put aside the need to be important and to fight for respect and they can begin to treat others gently. Children also can grow gentleness by reminding themselves that God loves others as much as He loves them and that the other person is always more important than winning (see Matthew 11:29; Romans 12:3; Philippians 4:5).

9. *Self-control* is doing what's right no matter how we feel. The "self" in self-control means we are required to work at it. Self-control involves choosing God's way—with the Holy Spirit's help. Aid children in growing self-control by encouraging them to memorize Bible verses that will fortify them when they're tempted to choose wrong; instead of trying to control their behavior yourself, let them know that you expect them to learn to control themselves (see Proverbs 25:28; Romans 8:8-9).

Pray regularly that God will help your children to grow His fruit. Encourage them to pray this for themselves, and point out when they're making progress. Explain that God doesn't expect us to grow the Spirit's fruit on our own; He is eager to help.

GOD WANTS YOU TO MATURE AND DEVELOP YOUR PERSONALITY.
Maturing is the processing of growing up, of becoming all we're meant to be. We're all meant to reflect God's character, but in unique ways that are colored by our personalities. Encourage your children's uniqueness,

but at the same time guide them to express their individuality in ways that are more and more Christlike: "Therefore, as God's chosen people, holy and dearly loved, clothe yourselves with compassion, kindness, humility, gentleness and patience. Bear with each other and forgive whatever grievances you may have against one another. Forgive as the Lord forgave you. And over all these virtues put on love, which binds them all together in perfect unity.

"Let the peace of Christ rule in your hearts, since as members of one body you were called to peace. And be thankful. Let the word of Christ dwell in you richly as you teach and admonish one another with all wisdom, and as you sing psalms, hymns and spiritual songs with gratitude in your hearts to God. And whatever you do, whether in word or deed, do it all in the name of the Lord Jesus, giving thanks to God the Father through him" (Colossians 3:12-17).

Personality is no excuse for immature or wrong behavior. For example, a child who has strong leadership traits does not have an excuse for disobedience; an imaginative child does not have an excuse for lying. You can help your children find godly, mature expressions of the personalities God has given them.

If your child has a take-charge personality type, explain that this doesn't give him or her permission to always take charge and tell people what to do. Others need opportunities to cultivate their leadership skills too. Help your assertive leader/achiever develop in his or her weaker areas, such as sensitivity to others.

If your child is a socially-oriented personality type, explain that he or she can't always be the life of the party. Much as they might like to, lighthearted fun-lovers must not invade others' space and make a joke of everything. They need to learn to deal with details and to be sensitive to those who prefer things quiet rather than loud and crazy.

Is your child a sensitive and caring personality? He or she may want to take care of everyone. Let your child know, however, that he or she can't make everyone happy. Sensitive caregivers need to learn to let people be themselves emotionally. They also need to develop their leadership skills, which they tend to avoid in case their decisions might upset someone.

If your child is an organized detail person, point out the upside of his giftedness. But remind him of the dangers of forcing others to be organized and insisting that everything be done in a certain way. Perfectionists need to learn how to relax, even when they don't know how things will turn out, and let others do things in new ways. They also need to develop their sense of fun and begin to see the big picture.

DOING ALL GOD WANTS YOU TO DO

CHURCH IS GOD'S IDEA. JESUS IS THE HEAD OF THE CHURCH. AT CHURCH YOU LEARN ABOUT GOD AND ENCOURAGE EACH OTHER TO FOLLOW JESUS.

Church is people. It's a community of Christians who meet together to learn about God, encourage one another, grow, and worship. God knew you and your children wouldn't be able to follow Him alone, so He gave you the church.

Jesus is the head of the church: "And God placed all things under his feet and appointed him to be head over everything for the church, which is his body, the fullness of him who fills everything in every way" (Ephesians 1:22-23). The church is His "bride." That means He's responsible for it. He loves His church and watches over it to make sure it benefits His children—including yours.

"But why do I have to go to church?" Your children need to understand why you're asking them to go and how church benefits them. Explain that there they learn about God, are part of a supportive group, and find good friends. It's not just your church; it's their church, their community: "Consequently, you are no longer foreigners and aliens, but fellow citizens with God's people and members of God's household, built on the foundation of the apostles and prophets, with Christ Jesus himself as the chief cornerstone. In him the whole building is joined together and rises to become a holy temple in the Lord. And in him you too are being built together to become a dwelling in which God lives by his Spirit" (Ephesians 2:19-22). They'll need help to truly connect with others there. Make it as easy as you can for them to get involved, to meet and spend time with people from church.

To help children see how church relates to their lives as a whole, make a point of mentioning church during the week. For example, recall something you heard during a sermon and explain how it might help you resolve a problem you're facing. Get together with another church family. Pray together about concerns listed in the church bulletin. Have a family meeting to decide how much to donate to a special church offering and how each family member might get involved.

Avoid simply going to church and leaving as quickly as you can. Stick around to talk with other adults and to meet the children in your kids' classes. Use this time to make connections for yourself and for your children.

On the way to church, pray together as a family that God will help you learn about Him and develop relationships in which you can both provide and receive support. On the way home, discuss what you learned. Rather than simply asking, "What did you do in Sunday school?" try to be specific. Ask whether your children had fun, what songs they sang, whether they learned anything surprising, what the Bible story was, and how the lesson might help them during the coming week.

GOD WANTS YOU TO UNDERSTAND WHAT A BLESSING PEOPLE AND GOOD RELATIONSHIPS ARE.

God's stipulated most important commandment is to love Him wholeheartedly, and the second greatest commandment (Mark 12:31) brings with it the second greatest blessing—good relationships with people of all ages. Being able to get along with all kinds of people—even those who are "different"—will benefit your children throughout their lives. If they really learn how to love others as they love themselves, nothing will hold them back.

Read together what the Bible says about relationships. For examples, see Proverbs 12:18; 15:1-2; 17:27; 20:3; 21:23; 29:8; Matthew 5:9; 7:12; James 3:3-13.

Teach your children how to forgive and to ask for forgiveness: "Bear with each other and forgive whatever grievances you may have against one another. Forgive as the Lord forgave you" (Colossians 3:13). If Ben hits Ryan, begin by dealing with Ben. Explain why hitting is wrong and have him ask for forgiveness. Then ask Ryan to forgive Ben. If Ryan refuses to forgive, explain that we always need to forgive as God has forgiven us. Avoid giving the impression, however, that we have to deny our hurt feelings in order to forgive. Feelings are valid and important; they need to be acknowledged and comforted. Still, God tells us to forgive.

Conflicts happen in all relationships. Help your children realize that what they do with conflict can be bad or good. To help them deal with disagreements in a way that enables everyone to feel cared for, try sharing the following conflict-resolution skills.

1. *Be an active listener.* Let others finish talking before you start. If you're planning your next words while the other person is talking, you're not listening. Look at the other person when he or she is speaking; try not to fidget or make disbelieving faces. Make sure you clearly understand the other person's point of view before you share your own. Tell the other person what you think he or she is saying. If you get it wrong, the other person can clear up the misunderstanding.
2. *Remember that your way isn't the only way.* The other person may be right!
3. *Stick to the issue.* Don't attack the other person personally or drag in past mistakes or disagreements.
4. *Use "I" statements instead of "you" statements.* Talk about how you feel

("I feel irritated when I hear knuckles cracking") instead of blaming the other person ("You make me mad when you crack your knuckles").

5. *Avoid "always" and "never" statements.* For example, saying, "Sometimes I feel you aren't listening to me" is less likely to cause problems than saying, "You never listen!"

6. *Choose your battles.* Some things aren't worth fighting over. And the person is always more important than the issue.

7. *Look for a win-win solution.* There doesn't have to be a winner and a loser. If you're creative, you can come up with a solution where everyone benefits.

GOD HAS TAUGHT YOU RIGHT FROM WRONG. HE DID THIS TO KEEP YOU SAFE AND TO GIVE YOU A GOOD LIFE.

In a world that tends to reject the idea of absolute truth, it can be tough to teach your children that some things are right or wrong in all places for all people. Fortunately, your job is made easier by the fact that right and wrong actions often have obvious consequences. Lying, for example, frequently leads to betrayal and broken relationships. Bragging can stir up jealousy. Living God's way, on the other hand, leads to trust, respect, generosity, kindness, love, and a great relationship with God. Choosing the right way pays off.

God didn't tell us to do things a certain way in order to be controlling or make us sad. He did it because He knows how life works best: " 'For I know the plans I have for you,' declares the LORD, 'plans to prosper you and not to harm you, plans to give you hope and a future' " (Jeremiah 29:11). Living God's way gives the greatest chance for a satisfying life: "Be careful to obey all these regulations I am giving you, so that it may always go well with you and your children after you, because you will be doing what is good and right in the eyes of the LORD your God" (Deuteronomy 12:28).

Help your children to see the why and the who behind the rules. Just knowing the rules gives no real motivation to keep them. Let's say, for example, that your daughter cries, "But I don't want to clean my room!"

Tell her that we clean our rooms because it's important to take care of our possessions, which then last longer.

Once your children understand the reason behind a rule, take them to the Ruler behind the reason: God. Behind every rule and reason in the Bible stands God and His character. In the case of room cleaning, you could point out that God owns all our possessions and entrusts them to our care. He also created the universe to operate in an orderly way; a clean room reflects that.

While following God's instructions does lead to the best kind of life, that kind of life isn't necessarily the easiest kind. Doing the right thing can get us in trouble here on earth. People have, after all, been killed for obeying God. Point out to your children that real success in this life is pleasing God—and we may not see the rewards until we're in heaven.

THE TEN COMMANDMENTS ARE GOOD GUIDELINES FOR LIFE.
The Ten Commandments (Exodus 20:1-17; Deuteronomy 5:6-21) are God's basic laws for life. You'll want to help your children memorize them and, more importantly, understand and follow them.

1. *No other gods:* This is the foundation of all the other commandments. Before anything else, your children need the right relationship with God in their hearts.
2. *Don't make or worship idols:* If God is first in your children's hearts, they won't have idols—anything that's more important to them than God is, anything to which they look for ultimate happiness.
3. *Don't misuse God's name:* God's name is to be used only with respect, because of who He is.
4. *Keep the Sabbath:* Genesis tells us that God created the world and everything in it in six days, and on the seventh (Sabbath) day He rested. He tells us to set apart a day of rest too.
5. *Honor your parents:* One way in which your children learn to know God and get along with people is by obeying you. This is the first step in God's growth process.

6. *Don't murder:* The heart of this commandment is to love one another. When we respect life as precious, we treat people as God wants them to be treated—instead of "murdering" them in our thoughts or actions (see Matthew 22:37-39).

7. *Don't commit adultery:* Some relationships are more important than others. In the family, the closest is between husbands and wives. Marriage is a picture of the relationship between people and God—one not to be cheapened or betrayed.

8. *Don't steal:* Stealing puts your own wants above the rights of others. It also shows that you aren't trusting God to meet your needs. Helping children not to steal flows from helping them trust God and respect others.

9. *Don't lie:* God is truth, so lying is wrong. If your children love people, they'll respect them by telling the truth to and about them.

10. *Don't covet:* Coveting isn't just wanting what we don't have; it's wanting what we have no right to—someone else's stuff. Coveting puts things before people and God.

When helping your children memorize these commandments, choose a Bible version they understand. You might try teaching them a song that covers all ten—make one up if necessary! Have your children copy the commandments, one each to an index card, then mix up the cards and see if the children can put them back in order. Hang a poster board in your child's room and write down the first commandment. When the child has memorized the first one, add the second. Keep going until he's mastered all ten.

Once your children have learned the commandments, have family members help each other to notice situations in which the commandments apply. When a family member sees such a situation, he or she can call out the number of the related commandment. For instance, if Sister grabs Brother's CD player because she feels entitled to it, one of you can say, "Number 10!"

Explain to your children that people can't keep all the commandments on their own. These rules were given by God to show people that they are sinners and need His forgiveness. But the commandments are a standard to strive for, and God can help your children keep them. Jesus made it possible for the commandments to be written on their hearts (Jeremiah 31:33; see also 1 Thessalonians 5:23-24).

GOD WANTS YOU TO SHARE YOUR FAITH.

Sharing our faith is simply telling others what God has done for us—from giving us eternal life to answering our prayers to changing our habits. Your children are "witnessing" whether they're talking about God or not. Their lives speak loudly about who they are and what God means to them: "Always be prepared to give an answer to everyone who asks you to give the reason for the hope that you have" (1 Peter 3:15).

Jesus left His disciples the job of telling everyone about Him and what He did. That's an assignment for you and your children, too: "Therefore go and make disciples of all nations, baptizing them in the name of the Father and of the Son and of the Holy Spirit, and teaching them to obey everything I have commanded you. And surely I am with you always, to the very end of the age" (Matthew 28:19-20).

Before encouraging your children to share their faith, make sure they understand the basics themselves. Then, to help children get used to the idea of talking about something they believe in, ask them to tell you about a favorite TV show, sport, hobby, or best friend. Note their enthusiasm and lack of self-consciousness. Then explain that sharing our faith is telling what we believe about Jesus and why. We don't need to be experts. We just need a personal, living relationship with God that's worth talking about.

Speak respectfully of nonbelievers so that your children will understand that they need to tell people about Jesus in a loving way. Explain that we need to respect other people's God-given right to decide for themselves, and not be pushy. Praying for others is a great idea, but the choice to accept or reject Jesus is theirs alone.

If children fear "witnessing" because they might not know the answer to a friend's question, assure them that they don't have to know all the answers. If a puzzling question comes up, they can feel free to say, "I don't know, but I can find out," and get help later from you, a book, or a teacher. Many people aren't convinced by "proofs" or arguments anyway. They want to see Christians who show real love, as Jesus did.

YOUNG EXPLORERS

Your seven-to-nine-year-old children are young explorers—navigating their way, with you and God's Word to help guide them. Enjoy these years. Post this chart to remind yourself how much new spiritual territory your young explorers can conquer in these exciting years.

Ages 7–9

KNOWING		LOVING	LIVING	
A. Who God Is	B. What God Has Done	C. You Can Have a Relationship with God	D. You Can Be All God Wants You to Be	E. You Can Do All God Wants You to Do
1. You can be sure that God is real. 2. There is only one God. 3. God exists in three Persons: Father, Son, and Holy Spirit. This is called the "Trinity." 4. God (Father, Son, and Holy Spirit) is eternal. 5. Jesus is both God and Man. 6. Nothing exists apart from God. 7. God's character is true, honest, loving, compassionate, generous, selfless, forgiving, merciful, trustworthy, faithful, just, impartial, and holy.	8. The Bible is true. It is God's Word, and you can trust it. 9. God made sure all stories in the Bible together tell the One Big Story. 10. The Bible you have is exactly what God wanted to give you. 11. God wants you to learn and study the Bible. 12. The world is full of sin. There is an enemy in the world (Satan). Not everyone obeys God. 13. Jesus died to save you from the penalty for sin. 14. Jesus defeated sin and Satan. 15. Jesus is the only way to God.	16. You read the Bible to learn about who God is (Father, Son, and Holy Spirit) and what He has done and is doing. 17. You can pray your own prayers with your parents. 18. Prayer benefits you in many ways. 19. Keep praying: Persistence, tests, and trials. 20. You can trust God and turn your life over to Him. 21. You should learn to seek God. 22. Jesus gives you peace.	23. God wants you to learn and grow and become like Jesus. 24. Growth is a learning process. 25. Your character should match God's character. 26. God wants you to develop your talents. 27. God wants you to develop the Fruit of the Spirit. 28. God wants you to mature and develop your personality.	29. Church is God's idea. Jesus is the head of the church. At church you learn about God and encourage each other to follow Jesus. 30. God wants you to understand what a blessing people and good relationships are. 31. God has taught you right from wrong. He did this to keep you safe and to give you a good life. 32. The Ten Commandments are good guidelines for life. 33. God wants you to share your faith.

PART 4

—

From Wrestling to Worship:
What Your 10-12-Year-Old Can Learn about God

CHAPTER 13

━ ━ ━ ━ ━ ━ ━ ━ ━

Helping Them Make
the Right Choices

Children ages 10 through 12 are moving into greater autonomy in many areas of their lives. They are making lots of decisions for themselves. They are also moving into an era of greater autonomy over their spiritual lives, so this is a crucial time for helping them choose to submit to God's authority. It's essential during these growing-up years for your 10-to-12-year-old children to learn what the Bible says about how they should live, what choices they need to make, and what God expects of them.

DEVELOPMENTAL DISTINCTIVES
Ages 10 to 12 make up a time of great personal growth and increasing independence.

PHYSICAL AND MENTAL DEVELOPMENT
At this age, children are working hard at growing up. A number of tasks begun earlier continue, such as internalizing values and forming

friendships. Peer groups become increasingly important. These children have a keen sense of loyalty, enjoy making things, want things to do, are on the move, like to compete, enjoy team games and hobbies, have good memories, and are collectors. They can think logically and reason about their experiences. They are capable of dealing with abstractions. They experience rapid changes in growth and development, continuing to gain two inches in height and six to seven pounds a year. They are still at the stage where they generally don't like the opposite sex. They show a marked increase in physical coordination and an increased attention span. They need extended physical activity as heart and lung capacity grow. They learn how to resolve conflict fairly and notice when their needs are different from those of others. This is a time to explore their abilities and talents and see where they fit.

> Children ages 10 through 12 are moving into greater autonomy, so this is a crucial time for helping them choose to submit to God's authority over their lives.

Emotions are relatively stable until the end of this stage, when they can swing wildly as hormones build and sexual development begins. Girls generally mature physically a year ahead of boys, often reaching puberty in elementary school. Both sexes are becoming conscious of their bodies. Lack of self-confidence grows along with self-consciousness and the deep longing for acceptance and approval. For this reason they may be tempted to associate with popular people—regardless of the morals of these people. They need your ongoing acceptance and affirmation. If they don't get it, they'll look for acceptance and affirmation elsewhere. They are shifting from being good because you say so to being good on their own.

During this time, it can be helpful to prepare them in advance for what puberty will bring: the changes in their bodies, emotional ups and downs, the importance of friends, greater independence, and the dangers of peer groups. It will seem like everything is changing, but assure them that your love and God's love are constant.

SPIRITUAL DEVELOPMENT

The main goal in raising children is to ensure that, by the time they leave home, they have incorporated God's values into their lives and have a fully developed and mature relationship with God. Ages 10 to 12 are important transition periods in their growth toward that goal. These children are moving from dependence to independence. Naturally, your involvement doesn't stop when they hit 13, but it changes. Your children realize, *I'm a person in my own right. These are my thoughts. This is my life. This is my faith.* They see the need to take ownership of developing their own spiritual life and being responsible for their walk with God.

These children are really beginning to think for themselves. They have a lot of information and are ready to make choices based on it. Your job is to help them learn to make the right choices. You need to begin letting go and allow them to test their wings and make decisions in the controlled, safe environment of home—especially about things that don't matter in the grand scheme of things, such as what hairstyle to have, how late to stay up on weekends, when to spend time with God, and so on. Knowing your standards and how you arrived at them will give them the rationale for making good choices. It can also help you, as these smaller things remind you that changes are necessary and are happening.

In addition, children need to know that the disciplines they are establishing will benefit them their whole lives—just as going to school will. They know that they need to learn and are aware of the benefits of good grades: they can go to college, become good at a profession, find fulfilling work, or start their own business. They may not always enjoy school or the process of learning, but they know why they need to be disciplined and study. Similarly, they can now understand that while there are occasions when spending time with God seems to have less immediate appeal than playing a video game, the long-term importance is far greater. Understanding this helps them develop their spiritual lives as they would a talent or skill they're excited about.

KEY WAYS TO PREPARE THEIR CHOICES

The snapshots that fill this section of your children's spiritual photo albums are chock-full of all kinds of things, from school to clubs to friends to church. Their lives are expanding and so are the "pictures" they take—they're beginning to include things from the wide world and show your children's growing experiences and confidence. You still appear in the background of some of the shots, but your presence is becoming less central. In fact, it's time to move purposefully out of the way.

Encourage them to take more responsibility by easing them into it. Even so, don't just let go and tell your children, for example, to have their own times with God. If you remove your involvement in their spiritual lives too soon or too suddenly, devotional times could stagnate or disappear. Instead, gradually give your children more and more rope. Encourage them to take increasing responsibility for your devotional times together. If you have been using the time just before bed as your time with God, then it has also become an important relational time between you and your child. Don't abandon it; change its function. Morph it gradually into a time to visit, to talk about what's happening in their lives, and to discuss what they want to pray about. You might pray for a few things together and then let them pray quietly about others. When they can get through the prayer time without input from you, or when they say, "I want to do it on my own," they are ready for you to pull back. That's a good sign. They're getting personal with God.

> The main goal in raising children is to ensure that, by the time they leave home, they have incorporated God's values into their lives and have fully developed a mature relationship with God.

Remind them of their times with God and help them plan them. You will need to help them make their times with God consistent, just as you remind them to brush their teeth: You don't stand over them while they brush but you help them to remember to do it and to be consistent.

Show your children how to find answers in the Bible. The same process of withdrawal and transition happens in all areas of their spiritual growth, such as Bible reading. They're too old for Bible storybooks, so replace them with age-appropriate full-text Bibles of their own. When they have questions, direct them to a part of the Bible that will help them. Let them choose what Bible books to read. You can offer suggestions, such as Genesis or one of the Gospels, or perhaps Esther or Ruth for girls. Read the same book independently, then discuss what you've read. Ask them what they learned and share what you got out of it. It's important for them to discover how to get direction for and insight from their reading. After all, the goal of Bible reading is learning and application. But don't force it. Trust God to work in their lives and speak to them.

Encourage their participation in church activities by making it easy for them to get there. Church is becoming increasingly important to children this age. They are getting more involved in church, attending extra meetings, helping out, joining clubs, going on trips or missions excursions, and making their key friends there. Church provides a wonderful, safe place for them to explore autonomy in their faith.

Let your children see what's outside the Christian bubble. They need to be exposed to other ideas and ways of thinking and believing so they'll know how to handle them. They need to begin to discern between cultural "truths" and God's truth, discover what to do with new ideas, and learn to compare them with Scripture. And they need to understand why Scripture is the standard.

Share with your children what you're learning. As your children grow older, your relationship with them changes into that of travelers on the same road sharpening one another. Ask them to pray about your concerns, such as work, and ask them what concerns of theirs they want you to pray for. Explain that you are growing with God together. Let them know that you value them as growing, maturing people. Then, when they finally leave home, they will be people who can speak into your life as you speak into theirs.

COMMON REFLECTIONS OF FAITH AT THIS AGE

By the time your children leave this stage and head for their teens, they will know who they are, how they fit into God's story, and what choices they're responsible for. They will have a history of good decision making and be comfortable with the idea that they have made and can make right choices and discipline themselves to have times with God. With this foundation they will grow into people who want to know and learn more about the Christian life, grow in their relationship with God, and take responsibility for it.

As your children move toward their teens, they face greater temptations. They must be ready to resist them and hang on to the truth. The key is for them to know that their relationship with God is the foundation and cornerstone of the rest of their lives. When they understand this, their view of life through their teen years will be molded by it. They will, with your ongoing help, be able to weather many storms and use the right tools to make good decisions.

CREATING A MEMORY MARKER: COMMITMENT

At each stage of your children's spiritual development, you've marked important times for them to remember—their infant dedication, the day they prayed to receive Christ as Savior, a special date night with you when you reaffirmed their knowledge of what it means to be saved. At this stage, you're on the brink of another spiritual "rite of passage"—their shift from young childhood to their teen years. At this time of their lives, they are often ready to make an informed, personally chosen commitment to God and His ways. Talk to them ahead of time about whether they are ready to make a serious commitment to follow God for the rest of their lives. This will deepen their commitment to obedience and a biblical lifestyle. When they are ready, create an event they'll remember. This will be especially important for those who were so young when they made their original commitment that they don't remember.

Some churches have a time, such as confirmation or baptism, Sunday school graduation, or official church membership, that offer a natural "Memory Marker" occasion for you and your family to celebrate. If your church doesn't have one, make a special occasion with friends and family for your children as they commit to follow God. Take pictures, buy a new outfit, have a special meal, give them something—a spiritual journal, a devotional book, a new Bible, a locket—to represent their new commitment.

THINGS ABOUT GOD THEY'RE READY TO LEARN

This chart shows the information your children are ready to learn now. As you ensure they have what they need to make informed choices, always bring the topic back to the practical: How does this affect their lives? What does this mean to them where they are now?

Ages 10–12

KNOWING		LOVING	LIVING	
A. Who God Is	B. What God Has Done	C. You Can Have a Relationship with God	D. You Can Be All God Wants You to Be	E. You Can Do All God Wants You to Do
1. Not everyone believes the truth about God, but there are ways you can respond to their objections. (Handling contrary opinions about God: basic apologetics; other religions)	2. God wants you to explore the One Big Story. 3. God put the Bible together in a fascinating way. 4. You need to learn how to study the Bible. 5. God lets His people serve Him and express their worship of Him in different ways. 6. God gave us an accurate record of His Son, Jesus. 7. God wants you to tell others about what Jesus has done. 8. Jesus will return as Judge and there will be a new heaven and a new earth.	9. You can pray on your own. 10. You can read the Bible on your own. 11. You can learn to worship God and Jesus on your own or in a group.	12. God wants you to choose to grow, learn, and seek His wisdom. 13. God's grace: You don't have to do it on your own. God is working in you by His Holy Spirit. 14. God wants you to find and follow His will for your life.	15. God wants you to choose to commit your entire life and everything you have to Him. 16. God wants you to choose His way because you love Him and want to be like Jesus. 17. God wants you to learn to seek and follow His Spirit's leading. 18. You need to learn how to resist Satan and temptation. 19. You need to get involved in church and find your place in the body of Christ.

CHAPTER 14

‒ ‒ ‒ ‒ ‒ ‒ ‒ ‒ ‒

Knowing

What Preteens Can Learn about God's Character and Actions

At each stage of your children's spiritual development, it's been foundational for them to understand God's character, especially by seeing what God has done and is doing. As your children build on these foundational truths, they'll come to see what happens when others reject these foundational truths. As the world grows wider, it's more important than ever for them to see how God's character and actions hold up under the scrutiny of criticism or of other religions.

UNDERSTANDING MORE ABOUT WHO GOD IS

NOT EVERYONE BELIEVES THE TRUTH ABOUT GOD—HANDLING CONTRARY OPINIONS.

At this stage, your children are internalizing what you've taught them about God, making it part of their own personal belief system. They've also noticed, however, that not everyone believes the same things: "The fool says in his heart, 'There is no God'" (Psalm 14:1). Friends, teachers, media—all will challenge your children's relationship with God and their understanding of who He is. You can help prepare them for these assaults so they won't be taken by surprise or be confused or deceived:

> "Now faith is being sure of what we hope for and certain of what we do not see. . . . And without faith it is impossible to please God, because anyone who comes to him must believe that he exists and that he rewards those who earnestly seek him" (Hebrews 11:1, 6).

At this stage, your children are internalizing what you've taught them about God, making it part of their own personal belief system.

To help your children sort out views of God, you may want to share the following definitions with them:

- *Monotheism:* Belief in one God. Christianity, Judaism, and Islam share this, but the latter two don't accept the idea that Jesus is God.
- *Polytheism:* Belief that there are many gods, or at least more than one.
- *Universalism:* Belief that all faiths lead to God. Many people with this view are offended by the Bible's position that Jesus is the only way to God.
- *Atheism:* Belief that there is no God. Many with this view would say that the universe and everything in it came to be by accident.
- *Pantheism:* Belief that the universe is God. Many with this view would say that God is not a Person, but the sum of all the forces of nature.
- *Agnosticism:* Belief that you can't know for sure whether God is real. Some with this view would say that faith—believing without absolute proof—is foolish.

Kids may find it easy to reject ideas like atheism or pantheism, but they may fall prey to more subtle distortions of who God is. For example, they may get the impression that God is the "Eye in the sky," watching and waiting for them to mess up—rather than Someone who is on their side, enjoying them and helping them to try again when they fail. Or they may fall prey to the opposite notion—that God doesn't care about sin and just wants everyone to be happy. To help children form a balanced, biblical view of God, keep bringing them back to what the Bible says about Him in verses like Romans 6:23; 2 Thessalonians 1:6; and 1 John 4:8.

Explain why it's important to believe what the Bible says about God. For example, if Jesus isn't God, He couldn't have been perfect or died to pay for our sins; He would have had to pay for His own. The result: no forgiveness or life in heaven with God after we die.

One of the challenges your children will face is the theory of evolution. They need to know that believing in a biblical view of creation is reasonable and based on evidence. Here are just a few faith-building facts you can share with them:

1. Evolutionists generally assume that single-cell creatures evolved into fish that crawled onto land and eventually evolved into humans. But even if the earth is four billion years old, as evolutionists say, many scientists realize this is not nearly long enough for even single-cell creatures to develop. Even with enough time, the odds of all the parts of a single-cell creature coming together by themselves in the right way to form life are from 1 in 1,060 to 1 in 1,040,000. And what about a human being, made of millions of cells and many interconnecting systems? The odds are impossible to calculate!

2. There's still no solid evidence of transitional creatures between reptiles and birds and between apelike animals and humans. "Missing link" discoveries have proven false. Some consider Heidelberg man, reconstructed from a jawbone, to be a missing link; but fully human natives of New Caledonia have the same jawbone.

3. Some people think that if God cannot be proven scientifically to ex-

ist, then He does not exist and there must be some other explanation for the universe. But even science assumes the existence of unseen subatomic particles simply because of their effects on their surroundings. Isn't it reasonable to believe God exists when His effects can be seen all around us?

4. Evolution or creation? Since none of us was present at the beginning, it's a matter of faith either way. Everyone believes "unprovable" things—some more reasonable than others. Based on the evidence, faith in God seems at least as reasonable as the alternative.

As you seek to counter false ideas about God, keep in mind three tips that can make your job easier:

1. Unless they indicate otherwise, assume your children are with you, believing what you've taught them.
2. Avoid force-feeding. Instead, watch for times when children are curious. Give them what they can handle and come back later when they're ready for more.
3. Help children find books, videos, and other resources that offer evidence for the biblical view. Not all the answers have to come directly from you. If children have trouble understanding the resources alone, explore them together.

UNDERSTANDING MORE ABOUT WHAT GOD HAS DONE

GOD WANTS YOU TO EXPLORE THE ONE BIG STORY. GOD PUT THE BIBLE TOGETHER IN A FASCINATING WAY.

By this time your children may understand what Jesus has done for them and may have received Him as Savior. If not, you'll want to review the Scriptures that point to their need for a Savior and how God has provided for that need.

Once children grasp and accept the basics, remind them that receiving Jesus is the beginning—the first step on the road to a fulfilling life and a wonderful relationship with God. Your goal now is for them to choose to be part of God's big story. They need to understand that story on a deeper level than they have before. You can help them do that by easing them into reading a full-text, age-appropriate Bible of their own. They're ready for the whole thing: "Everything must be fulfilled that is written about me in the Law of Moses, the Prophets and the Psalms" (Luke 24:44; see also Matthew 22:40 and Luke 16:31).

> Once children grasp and accept the basics, remind them that receiving Jesus is the beginning—the first step on the road to a fulfilling life and a wonderful relationship with God.

Since the Bible can be overwhelming, especially if we aren't sure how to approach it, you can make things easier by telling your children how the Bible is structured. You may even want to describe the Bible as a whole library of books. Like a library, it's organized into sections. First, it's divided into two main parts—the Old Testament and the New Testament.

The Old Testament contains 39 books:

- *Five books of the Law* (Genesis to Deuteronomy)—Creation, Adam and Eve and the first sin, Noah, the patriarchs (Abraham to Jacob), Joseph, Moses and the Exodus, the Israelites' wandering in the desert, and the rules God gave them.
- *Twelve books of history* (Joshua to Esther)—the conquering and settling of Canaan, the judges, the kings of Israel and Judah, what happened when the kingdoms were conquered and taken captive by Assyria and Babylon, how the Jews came back to the land God promised them, and how Esther saved them all.
- *Five books of poetry* (Job to Song of Songs)—instructions for life and wisdom about relationships with God.
- *Five major prophets* (Isaiah to Daniel) and *12 minor prophets* (Hosea to Malachi)—the words and actions of some of the prophets God sent to Israel and Judah during the time of the kings, during the exile in Babylon, and during the first century

after the Jews returned to their land. They're called "major" and "minor" because of the lengths of the books, not their importance.

The New Testament contains 27 books:

- *Four Gospels* or "good news" books (Matthew, Mark, Luke, and John)—separate accounts of Jesus, each with a different emphasis.
- *One book of history* (Acts)—what happened after Jesus returned to heaven, how the news about Him spread through the Roman world, and how the church began.
- *Thirteen letters or epistles* (Romans to Philemon)—explanations of the Christian faith and instructions on how to follow Jesus, most of which were written by the apostle Paul.
- *Eight general letters or epistles* (Hebrews to Jude)—guidance on Christian living written by other early church leaders. These letters are "general" because they weren't addressed to any particular person or church.
- *One book of prophecy* (Revelation)—a vision the apostle John had while a prisoner on the island of Patmos; it talks about what will happen in the end, including the return of Jesus.

To help your children remember the library layout of the Bible, tell them that the Old Testament books are "5-12-5-5-12": 5 books of law, 12 books of history, 5 books of poetry, 5 major prophets, and 12 minor prophets. The New Testament books are "4-1-13-8-1": 4 Gospels, 1 book of history, 13 epistles to specific churches, 8 general epistles, and 1 book of prophecy.

YOU NEED TO LEARN HOW TO STUDY THE BIBLE.

As your children begin to read full-text Bibles, you can introduce them to the idea of studying God's Word. You don't need to turn them into Bible scholars. The important thing is that they discover that the Bible really contains answers to their questions, and that digging into it will help them live the most satisfying lives: "Now the Bereans were of more noble character than the Thessalonians, for they received the message with great eagerness and examined the Scriptures every day to see if what Paul said was true" (Acts 17:11).

There's more than one way to study the Bible. Tell your children about the following methods. In fact, why not try them yourself and let your children watch and learn?

- *Topical studies* help you discover what the Bible says on a certain subject, such as love or forgiveness.
- *Word studies* involve looking up verses in which a certain word, such as *grace* or *worship* is used, so that you can get a clearer picture of what it means.
- *Character studies* help you find out all you can about a Bible character like David or Deborah.
- *Book studies* focus on one book in the Bible, such as Ruth or Galatians, and explore what it means and how it applies to today.

Show your children tools like the following that can help with Bible study. If you don't have these, try borrowing some from the church library or a friend.

- *Concordance:* This is an index of most words used in the Bible and where to find them. Many Bibles have a simplified one in the back. This tool is especially useful when you know part of a verse but not where to find it or when you're doing a word study.
- *Topical index:* This reference lists verses by subject—even those that don't use a particular word. For example, if you're studying forgiveness, a topical index will take you to the story of the Prodigal Son, which is about forgiveness but doesn't use the word.
- *Cross-references:* These are the numbers and notes found in the

margins or center column in many Bibles. They help you to find related verses.

- *Bible dictionary:* This gives you the meanings of words used in the Bible, plus background material on biblical people and places.

- *Bible commentary:* This tool comments on verses and sections, helping you understand the context of the passage, the author's original meaning, and how it might apply today. Some Bibles have brief commentaries at the bottom of the pages; other commentaries are in separate volumes.

- *Book introductions:* Many Bibles introduce each Bible book with background information (such as who wrote it, when, and why) and an overview or outline of the book.

- *Bible atlas or maps:* In the back of many Bibles—and in separate books—are maps that help you see where the Bible's events took place.

To encourage kids to start searching the Scriptures for themselves, challenge them to find out on their own what the Bible says about a situation they're facing—a rocky friendship, for instance, or a decision about how to spend some money. If they get stuck, help them out. When they're done, ask them to share with you what they found.

The ancient names of the Bible's countries and cities, even when shown on maps, may seem like imaginary places to your children. Using a contemporary atlas, point out these places on modern maps. Babylon, for example, seems far, far away; Iraq seems much more immediate.

GOD LETS HIS PEOPLE SERVE HIM AND EXPRESS THEIR WORSHIP OF HIM IN DIFFERENT WAYS.

Christians generally agree on the basic doctrines of the Apostles' Creed. But your children will encounter many differences among churches, and they may wonder why. You can help clear up the confusion and guide children to appreciate the freedom God gives us to honor Him in a variety of ways.

THE APOSTLES' CREED

I believe in God, the Father almighty, creator of heaven and earth.

I believe in Jesus Christ, His only Son, our Lord. He was conceived by the power of the Holy Spirit and born of the Virgin Mary. He suffered under Pontius Pilate, was crucified, died, and was buried. He descended into hell. On the third day He rose again. He ascended into heaven and is seated at the right hand of the Father. He will come again to judge the living and the dead.

I believe in the Holy Spirit, the holy Christian church, the communion of saints, the forgiveness of sins, the resurrection of the body, and life everlasting.

You can help your children distinguish the essentials of the Christian faith from the way Christians express and celebrate that faith. Explain that God made people with a great variety of personalities and tastes. Naturally, this comes through in how Christians serve and worship Him. Some churches emphasize certain parts of the Christian life—sharing one's faith, studying the Bible, helping the poor, etc. Churches also tend to emphasize certain forms of worship, based on tradition and preference—choosing one kind of music over another, dressing in a particular way, moving or not moving to show their feelings, and so forth.

Try taking a family field trip to a church unlike your own, so that your children can experience another form of worship. Then ask, "How might the things they did be expressions of their love for God? How is that church like ours?"

It's important to focus on the things Christians have in common. But feel free to teach your children about the things that make your church unique, too, so that they can fully participate in your worship service and the rest of your church's program: "Make every effort to keep the unity of the Spirit through the bond of peace. There is one body and one Spirit—just as you were called to one hope when you were called—one Lord, one faith, one baptism; one God and Father of all, who is over all and through all and in all" (Ephesians 4:3-6).

GOD GAVE US AN ACCURATE RECORD OF HIS SON, JESUS.

We shouldn't be surprised when those who want to undermine Christianity attack Jesus. After all, He's the cornerstone of the Christian faith! Your children will face those who say that Jesus never really lived or that He wasn't really God. You can help prepare them for this by making sure their faith in Him is solidly grounded.

Can you "prove" to your children that Jesus really lived? Perhaps not. But you can offer some convincing evidence. If you like, read the following to them or share it in your own words.

1. *Eyewitness accounts:* The Bible is our main source for information about Jesus. Is the Bible accurate? It's been shown to tell the truth about so much else that you can be confident it tells the truth about Jesus. Those who wrote the Gospels were convinced that what they'd seen and heard was real: "We did not follow cleverly invented stories when we told you about the power and coming of our Lord Jesus Christ, but we were eyewitnesses of his majesty" (2 Peter 1:16; see also John 21:24-25). Their books were written when others who'd been with Jesus were still alive. If the Gospel writers had been telling lies, these others would certainly have exposed them—but they didn't: "God raised him from the dead, freeing him from the agony of death, because it was impossible for death to keep its hold on him. . . . God has raised this Jesus to life, and we are all witnesses of the fact. . . . Therefore let all Israel be assured of this: God has made this Jesus, whom you crucified, both Lord and Christ" (Acts 2:24, 32, 36).

2. *Extrabiblical sources:* The Bible isn't the only book that mentions Jesus. Others who wrote not long after He lived show that He was a real, historical person. Flavius Josephus, a Jewish historian who lived around A.D. 70, mentioned Jesus, saying that He was condemned to death by Pilate and then appeared alive again on the third day. Josephus also mentioned Jesus when he told how James,

Jesus' brother, was killed. Then there's a letter from a leading Roman, Tacitus (around A.D. 112), mentioning that Jesus was put to death under Pilate. And some Jewish teachers of the time referred to Jesus or Yeshua.

At this stage, many children want evidence to back up the claim that Jesus is God—especially if they've encountered peers who disagree. Here are some thoughts you may want to offer:

1. *Jesus claimed He was God.* As C. S. Lewis wrote, there are only three things you can believe about Jesus' claim: He is who He says He is (God and Lord); He was a liar who knew He was lying; or He just thought He was telling the truth when He wasn't—in other words, He was a lunatic.

   Lots of people would agree that Jesus was a great teacher of right and wrong. If He was, He couldn't be a liar. Was He crazy? None of His other words or actions suggest that He was. The only possibility left is that He's who He claims to be—Lord.

2. *Jesus rose from the dead.* Jesus died, yet three days later He was alive again. What happened? The Romans made sure Jesus was dead. His body was wrapped in cloths with spices, which made the grave clothes stick to the body. They would be very difficult to remove. He was placed in a burial chamber cut into solid rock, its one exit covered by a huge stone that took several people to move. Soldiers guarded the tomb; they knew that sleeping on the job brought a death penalty.

   Yet three days later, the tomb was empty. The huge stone had been moved away from the tomb; the grave clothes were empty as if Jesus' body had passed right through them. The soldiers were bribed to say they'd fallen asleep, yet they were not punished for it. Nor were the disciples punished for stealing Jesus' body. More than 500 people saw Jesus alive after His death. And the disciples were never the same, changing from scared people hiding from the authorities to bold people who were willing to suffer beatings and even death. Knowing that Jesus rose from the dead helped them to be bold.

How do we know Jesus is the Messiah? One way is through the predictions that Jesus fulfilled—60 major Old Testament prophecies about the Messiah! Here are some you may want to point out to your children:

PROPHECY	OT REFERENCE	NT FULFILLMENT
The Messiah would be or have:		
The Son of God	Psalm 2:7; Proverbs 30:4	Matthew 3:17; Luke 1:32
Born of virgin	Isaiah 7:14	Matthew 1:18-25; Luke 1:26-35
Born in Bethlehem	Micah 5:2	Matthew 2:1; Luke 2:4-6
From tribe of Judah	Genesis 49:10	Matthew 1:2; Luke 3:33-34
Betrayed	Psalm 41:9	John 13:18, 21, 26-27
Beaten	Isaiah 50:6	Matthew 26:67; 27:26, 30
Crucified	Psalm 22:1, 6-18; 69:21	Matthew 27:34-50; John 19:28-30
Bones unbroken	Psalm 34:20	John 19:31-37
Pierced	Psalm 22:16; Zechariah 12:10	John 19:34, 37
Raised from dead	Psalm 16:1	Luke 24:1-12; Acts 13:35-37

GOD WANTS YOU TO TELL OTHERS ABOUT WHAT JESUS HAS DONE. Many Christians are intimidated by the idea of witnessing. But when Jesus is an important part of your children's lives, talking about Him will be as natural and easy as talking about a best friend. Rather than treating sharing their faith as a separate "job" Christians are supposed to do, encourage kids to see it as a way of letting their good feelings about God overflow into other people's lives: "Therefore go and make disciples of all nations, baptizing them in the name of the Father and of the Son and of the Holy Spirit, and teaching them to obey everything I have commanded you. And surely I am with you always, to the very end of the age" (Matthew 28:19-20).

The best way to help your children tell others about Jesus is to help them fall in love with Him: "In your hearts set apart Christ as Lord. Always be prepared to give an answer to everyone who asks you to give the reason for the hope that you have. But do this with gentleness and respect" (1 Peter 3:15). Few have an urge to share knowledge that's strong enough to overcome shyness or fear. But most who are in love find it easy to talk about the object of their affection.

"I can't tell people about Jesus," your children might say. "They'll get mad if I say Jesus is the only way and their religion is wrong." How can you reply?

Help your children to understand that Christianity isn't exclusive and narrow-minded—it's inclusive and welcoming. "Membership" in most religions is available to a select few—those who perform certain tasks to earn God's favor, who are born into a certain culture, or who otherwise fit a certain profile. Christianity is the only faith that says you can do nothing to earn heaven—yet your entrance can be guaranteed! Jesus clearly stated the way: "I am the way and the truth and the life. No one comes to the Father except through me" (John 14:6).

This does not exclude people; it includes everyone. No matter where you're from, what you look like, how smart or hardworking or lazy you are, you're welcome. All you have to do is accept God's free gift of forgiveness, delivered to you through Jesus' death. Make sure your children understand that He is the wide-open door to heaven through which anyone can enter and through which everyone must enter. We don't need to "fight" other religions; we just need to tell people the truth and give them the chance to meet Jesus.

Some children, feeling anxious about whether their friends will go to heaven, may try to pressure those friends into becoming Christians. Encourage your children to be gentle in the way they talk about Jesus. They need to be ready, respectful, humble, and caring. No matter what the other person's response is, he or she deserves to be treated with kindness. Each person has a God-given right to choose to follow Jesus or not. Arguments, demands, and pressure don't bring people into God's kingdom; loving them, respecting them, and answering their questions can. Urge your children to trust God to help them tell others about Him and to leave the results in His hands.

Even the most enthusiastic child needs knowledge and answers to back up his or her zeal. Show your children where to find Bible verses explaining how to accept Jesus. There are many ways to explain the gospel; encourage kids to tell the story of their journey with Jesus in their own words.

JESUS WILL RETURN AS JUDGE AND THERE WILL BE A NEW HEAVEN AND A NEW EARTH.

Children are often drawn to—and confused by—the prophetic parts of the Bible. As they read their Bibles or listen in Sunday school, your children will encounter Ezekiel, Daniel, Revelation, and other sections that are difficult to understand. They may be even more confused when they learn that Christians interpret these writings in different ways. You can help reduce the confusion—and assure your children that the most important thing to know about the future is that God has a wonderful plan for us, a plan that includes the return of Jesus: "For the Lord himself will come down from heaven, with a loud command, with the voice of the archangel and with the trumpet call of God, and the dead in Christ will rise first. After that, we who are still alive and are left will be caught up together with them in the clouds to meet the Lord in the air. And so we will be with the Lord forever. Therefore encourage each other with these words" (1 Thessalonians 4:16-18).

When children ask what prophetic passages mean, use the opportunity to explain a couple of basic guidelines for interpreting the Bible:

- *Start with the straightforward.* God presented clearly what He really wants us to know. Things about the future that are less urgent to know He presents symbolically. It's better to first read "basic" Scriptures that deal with the end times (like Matthew 24:1-5 and 1 Thessalonians 4:13–5:11) and *then* move to more symbolic passages (such as Revelation and Daniel 7–12), rather than the other way around.

- *Look for the big idea.* The question to ask about tough passages is "What's the main point?" The main point of Revelation, for instance, is "Jesus is coming back. Be ready!"

How can you deal with differing views of the end times? Let children know that Christians have various opinions about the meaning of certain Scriptures, especially those that contain symbolic language or that don't go into great detail about an issue. Let them know your viewpoint. Help them understand that the principles are more important than the details, and that God's Spirit will help them understand what they need to know. As for prophecy, explain that none of us will completely understand it—until it happens: "Now, brothers, about times and dates we do not need to write to you, for you know very well that the day of the Lord will come like a thief in the night" (1 Thessalonians 5:1-2).

CHAPTER 15

— — — — — — — — —

Loving

Your Preteen's Enriched Relationship with God

The Lord who began His good work in your children has promised to continue it (Philippians 1:6). During these ages from 10 to 12, your children may grow deeper in their dependent and submitted relationship to Him.

DEVELOPING A FRIENDSHIP WITH GOD

YOU CAN PRAY ON YOUR OWN.

Keep praying and reading the Bible with your children as long as they want you to. There's no need to rush them into doing these things alone. These times together can be important to parents and children—and forcing children to go solo before they're ready could cause them to flounder and give up. But at this stage most children are able to pray their own prayers, though you'll probably want to be on the scene in the early years of this age range to help them be consistent and to offer input when necessary. Eventually children may want to pray silently. This usually shows they're getting personal with God and can talk to Him about things they're uncomfortable talking with anyone else about. It's a good sign. In time they'll want you to let them pray entirely on their own.

Take your children back to God's Word, the Bible, to revisit what God has instructed us about prayer. One important command is to pray  continually: "Be joyful always; pray continually; give thanks in all circumstances, for this is God's will for you in Christ Jesus" (1 Thessalonians 5:16-18). The Bible also tells us we can pray during good times and bad ones: "Is any one of you in trouble? He should pray. Is anyone happy? Let him sing songs of praise. Is any one of you sick? He should call the elders of the church to pray over him and anoint him with oil in the name of the Lord. And the prayer offered in faith will make the sick person well; the Lord will raise him up. If he has sinned, he will be forgiven. Therefore confess your sins to each other and pray for each other so that you may be healed. The prayer of a righteous man is powerful and effective" (James 5:13-16).

As for how they can shape their prayers, encourage them to start a prayer by praying about prayer! It's helpful to make prayer itself the first topic of a prayer. Encourage your children to begin by thanking God for hearing them and asking Him to help them pray as He wants them to. This "meeting to plan the meeting" prepares the heart.

At this stage most children are able to pray their own prayers.

You might encourage children to pause after each topic of prayer. This helps them slow down and think about what they're doing, and it reminds them that God is interested and involved in the conversation. Pausing at the end of a prayer gives them a chance to add anything else that comes to mind.

Share with your 10-to-12-year-old things that you've learned in your own prayer life, too.

YOU CAN READ THE BIBLE ON YOUR OWN.

It's time for a rite of passage! If your children don't have full-text Bibles of their own, take them to a Christian bookstore and let them help choose one. Their involvement will increase their sense of ownership and, ultimately, their willingness to read. If possible, steer them toward Bibles designed for preteens or teenagers, appropriate for their reading level, containing simple notes and reference tools.

Remind your children that reading their Bible regularly and thinking about what it says is God's idea: "Do not let this Book of the Law depart from your mouth; meditate on it day and night, so that you may be careful to do everything written in it. Then you will be prosperous and successful" (Joshua 1:8). God came up with that idea because He knows so well what they need. God loves His children so much that He wants to point them safely in all the ways they should go: "Your word is a lamp to my feet and a light for my path" (Psalm 119:105).

If your children are wondering where to start in that daunting full-text Bible, you might hand them this list—the "First Find Plan"—which points them to the books of the Bible that can provide a good overview of the One Big Story of Scripture:

1. Beginnings: Genesis
2. Forming a Nation: Exodus
3. Jesus' Story: Luke
4. The Church Begins: Acts
5. Practical Living: James

Once your children have completed the "First Find Plan" or a similar introduction to Bible reading, try having them move on to the "Treasure Trove Plan." You may want to photocopy this list, have your children keep it in their Bibles, and encourage them to check off the passages as they read.

Old Testament
Beginnings: Genesis 1–50
Forming a Nation: Exodus 1–40
Israel in the Desert: Numbers 8–27
Following God and Taking Over: Deuteronomy 6–7; 34
Conquest of the Promised Land: Joshua 1–10; 24
Unusual Judges: Judges 1–7; 13–16
Loyalty and Reward: Ruth
Saul's Fall; David, Fugitive Hero: 1 Samuel 1–21; 23–31
David Gets the Kingdom: 2 Samuel 5–7
Praise and Dedication: Psalm 23; 32; 100; 103; 130; 139
Solomon's Wisdom, Riches, and Wives: 1 Kings 3–5; 8–11
Prophets, Kings, and Other Things: 2 Kings 2–5; 7; 12; 18–20; 22–24
Messiah's Astonishing Mission: Isaiah 53
Fatal Fall of Jerusalem: Jeremiah 52:1-16
Daniel, Courageous Captive: Daniel 1–6
King Cyrus Lets Jews Return: 2 Chronicles 36:22-23
Rebuilding Altar and Temple: Ezra 1; 3; 6
Rebuilding Jerusalem's Walls: Nehemiah 1–8
Queen Saves the Day: Esther 1–10

New Testament
Jesus' Story: Luke 1–24
Jesus, God's Son: John 1–21
Witness to the World: Acts 1–28
Sins and a Savior: Romans 1–8; 12–14
Life in the Body: 1 Corinthians 12–14
Earth and Heaven: 2 Corinthians 4–5
Giving: 2 Corinthians 9
Real Freedom: Galatians 5–6

Unity, Goodness, Obedience, and Armor: Ephesians 4–6
Follow the Leader: Philippians 2–4
Pleasing God: 1 Thessalonians 3–4
Love God, Not Money: 1 Timothy 6
God's Prisoner Gives Advice: 2 Timothy 2–4
Do What's Good: Titus 3
The Faith Hall of Fame: Hebrews 11
Holiness and Hard Times: 1 Peter 1–4
The Day of the Lord: 2 Peter 3
Practical Living: James 1–5
Love God and Others: 1 John 1–5
Warnings and Rewards: Revelation 1–3; 20–22

If children express confusion about what they're reading, look together for answers in a Bible commentary or Bible dictionary. Make sure their Bible translation is easy to read. Remind them to pray before they read the Bible that God will give them understanding and wisdom and continue to teach them.

YOU CAN LEARN TO WORSHIP GOD AND JESUS ON YOUR OWN OR IN A GROUP.

What's worship? Children need to know that it takes many forms but boils down to one thing: giving of yourself to God in response to who He is. In worship we praise God honestly from our hearts, with our whole lives: "God is spirit, and his worshipers must worship in spirit and in truth" (John 4:24). Our obedient choices are also worship: "Therefore, I urge you, brothers, in view of God's mercy, to offer your bodies as living sacrifices, holy and pleasing to God—this is your spiritual act of worship" (Romans 12:1). Worship may happen in a group setting or when we're alone—anytime, anyplace. Getting together with other Christians to worship, however, can encourage us

157

to give more of ourselves to God—and it makes a visible statement to the rest of the world that God is truly worth praising.

To help kids understand how worship works, you might describe worship this way: Worship is like a loop, a circle. It starts with God. We  learn about God and realize we can trust Him: He keeps His promises, knows everything, can do anything, is everywhere, and always loves us. That makes us feel like praising and thanking Him and trusting Him with more of our lives. When we let Him take charge of more of our lives, He changes us, making us more like Jesus. When that happens, our praise comes from even deeper inside. We get together with others and tell how wonderful God is. This helps our trust in Him get even stronger, which leads us to greater worship. And on it goes; we get closer to God and worship Him more, which brings us even closer.

Your children may wonder why people worship God in different ways using various styles of music, postures, phrases, etc. Explain that each person is different and has a different relationship with God, so it makes sense that people would express that relationship in ways that fit who they are. Churches have different personalities and traditions too. What worship looks like is not as important as what's going on inside each person—something only God can know for sure.

When your children join you in your adult worship service, try to emphasize attitude over outward conformity. For example, if your church has a long worship service, kids might not be able to concentrate and participate the whole time. If their concentration is dwindling, suggest that they ask for God's help to focus; then they can sit quietly and wait, without distracting others. It's far better for them to worship from their hearts for five minutes than to just go through the motions for an hour. In addition, encourage them to worship along with the songs that are meaningful to them. If some lyrics are over their heads, tell kids that they may sit or stand quietly during those songs and talk to God in their hearts. After the service, explain the lyrics so that children can join in next time.

Show your children how God can be worshiped outside of a church service. Give them a tape or CD featuring praise music, and encourage them to listen to it on their own with a worshipful attitude. Take on a service project as a family—cleaning up a local park, serving food at a rescue mission, washing a disabled person's car—and explain how our work can fit the worship definition of "giving of yourself to God in response to who He is."

CHAPTER 16

--- --- --- --- --- --- --- --- ---

Living

How Preteens Can Live Out Their Faith

In this era of increasing independence and self-direction, it becomes more important than ever for your child to choose, day by day, to live for God. All believers, young and old, live out their faith by *being* God's much-loved children and by *doing* what pleases Him. At this stage, your preteens will exercise more autonomy over their being and doing!

BEING ALL GOD WANTS YOU TO BE

GOD WANTS YOU TO CHOOSE TO GROW, LEARN, AND SEEK HIS WISDOM.

Can you *make* your children grow spiritually? Not really. Even God doesn't force anyone to seek Him or obey Him. It's a choice God has left to each person. In Romans, the apostle Paul urged believers to offer God their obedient actions, exercising their own will to choose to live for God: "Therefore, I urge you, brothers, in view of God's mercy, to offer your bodies as living sacrifices, holy and pleasing to God—this is your spiritual act of worship. Do not conform any longer to the pattern of this world, but be transformed by the renewing of your mind. Then you will be able to test and approve what God's will is—his good, pleasing and perfect will" (Romans 12:1-2).

> **Even though you can't make spiritual choices for your children, you can guide them toward choosing to be what God wants them to be—and allowing God to work in them to change them.**

Even though you can't make these spiritual choices for your children, still you can guide them toward choosing to be what God wants them to be—and allowing God to work in them to change them. You can do this by pointing out the benefits of spiritual growth, noting real-life examples of people who are growing, and showing your children how to get started. Assure them that growth is a lifelong process—a journey toward getting closer to God and becoming more like Jesus: "Do you not know that in a race all the runners run, but only one gets the prize? Run in such a way as to get the prize. Everyone who competes in the games goes into strict training. They do it to get a crown that will not last; but we do it to get a crown that will last forever. Therefore I do not run like a man running aimlessly; I do not fight like a man beating the air. No, I beat my body and make it my slave so that after I have preached to others, I myself will not be disqualified for the prize" (1 Corinthians 9:24-27).

Help your children notice the people around them who are modeling the life of faith. Point out people in your church whose lives show the benefits of living for God. For example, a business owner may have prospered by earning a reputation for honesty. A retired missionary may have the satisfaction of knowing that he or she helped people find the way to heaven. A teenager may have enjoyed a summer trip to build houses in Central America. Give your children biblical examples of people who pursued God, such as David and Paul.

Come alongside your children and grow with them. Let them see you in the process of becoming more of the person God wants you to be. Apologize to your children when you make mistakes with them; it's a powerful lesson! When you apologize, try saying something like "I'm learning too. I'm asking God to change me and make me a better parent so I'll do better next time. I know I'm not perfect; I'm on the road to becoming a little more like Jesus. That's what God wants for all of us."

The Bible contains a wealth of verses about growing spiritually, seeking God, and not giving up. Here are some passages you may want to urge your children to memorize and meditate on: Psalm 25:4-5; 42:1-2; Philippians 2:12-13; 3:7-11, 13-14; Colossians 3:1-4, 5-17; 2 Timothy 2:15; Hebrews 6:1 and 12:1.

GOD'S GRACE: YOU DON'T HAVE TO DO IT ON YOUR OWN. GOD IS WORKING IN YOU BY HIS HOLY SPIRIT.

"Being a Christian is just too hard!" If your children feel that way, they'll appreciate the truth that we don't have to live the Christian life under our own power. Let them know that their part is mainly to cooperate with what God wants to do in their lives. He's right there, ready to help them become more like His Son: "Being confident of this, that he who began a good work in you will carry it on to completion until the day of Christ Jesus" (Philippians 1:6).

Point out to children that if they've received Jesus as Savior, God is with them continuously through His Spirit who teaches them from His Word, reminds them of His way, and gives them strength to make the right choices when they ask for it. God is for them, cheering them on, helping them grow to the next step.

When children do the wrong thing and feel guilty about it, they may wonder whether trying to follow Jesus is a lost cause. Assure them that God is never surprised by our mistakes or sins. If anything, He works to bring these into the open so that we know about them and can deal with them. God is there when we blow it; the best person to talk to right then is God Himself, as we ask Him to forgive us and to help us obey Him more completely: "No temptation has seized you except what is common to man. And God is faithful; he will not let you be tempted beyond what you can bear. But when you are tempted, he will also provide a way out so that you can stand up under it" (1 Corinthians 10:13; see also 15:10).

Does teaching your children seem like an overwhelming task? Just as they're not alone, neither are you! The responsibility for training your children spiritually is not solely on your shoulders. You teach them truths about God, modeling those truths as well as you can, and God works them into your children's hearts and lives. It's a cooperative process. Remember that God loves your children, and He knows exactly how to guide them.

Children may be confused over how much of the Christian life is up to them and how much is up to God. Explain that God doesn't do it all, moving us around and talking through us as if we were ventriloquist's dummies. God is more like a coach, ready to help us learn how to be and what to do. We can choose to cooperate with Him or not. God helps us love, for instance, but doesn't do it for us. That has to come from our hearts.

GOD WANTS YOU TO FIND AND FOLLOW HIS WILL FOR YOUR LIFE.

God has a plan for each of your children—a perfect match for the talents, gifts, and personality He's given each child: "The LORD will fulfill his purpose for me" (Psalm 138:8).

How do your children discover that plan? A little at a time! Knowing God's will starts with making right choices day by day. Each day we need to ask God what He has for us to do, then follow Him in that direction. If we're seeking a close relationship with God and are obeying Him, He'll lead us into what we're best suited for—what we'll enjoy and find fulfilling: "Delight yourself in the LORD and he will give you the desires of your heart. Commit your way to the LORD; trust in him and he will do this" (Psalm 37:4-5).

What does it mean to be a success? Do your children think that fame or money should be their goal? Help them see that real success comes from doing what God has designed us to do, even if our specific tasks change from time to time. Point out examples of Christians in your church who are serving God as homemakers, attorneys, artists, janitors—paid or unpaid, well-known or not. If possible, arrange for your children to spend time with a few of these people, finding out how they found their niches and how they continue to seek God's direction for their futures.

Ask your children, "What do you want to be when you grow up?" You'll probably get job-oriented answers; these are fine, but encourage kids to think outside the box, too. What do they want to be? What qualities do they hope to have when they're adults? Use this activity to remind children that God has a plan for the kind of people He wants us to be—not just for the things He wants us to do.

How can you help point your children toward the occupation, career, or ministry that's right for them? Encourage them to write down a list of "seeds" they think God may have planted in them—their personality type, talents and gifts, likes and wants. These seeds may give clues to what your children will be most fulfilled by doing one day. In the meantime, let them explore a variety of activities so they can find out what they enjoy and are good at. Urge them to pray for help to make the right choices. Remind them that God promises to give wisdom to those who ask (James 1:5).

DOING ALL GOD WANTS YOU TO DO

GOD WANTS YOU TO CHOOSE TO COMMIT YOUR ENTIRE LIFE AND EVERYTHING YOU HAVE TO HIM.

More than once Jesus said it was better to lose your life for His sake than to gain the world: "Whoever finds his life will lose it, and whoever loses his life for my sake will find it" (Matthew 10:39; see also Matthew 16:25; Mark 8:35; Luke 9:24; 17:33; and John 12:25). Purposely "losing your life"—putting aside your own wants in favor of God's agenda—is hardly something that comes naturally to most of us, no matter how old we are.

But Jesus said doing this is better than gaining the whole world! You can help your children see why. Explain that turning their lives over to God is more rewarding than running things on their own, because they can trust Him to take better care of them than they can themselves.

Help them know how to do this, too—by surrendering their lives to God every day, even minute by minute when necessary. They can learn to let Him be Lord in reality, not just in name.

"Losing your life" for the sake of Jesus doesn't always lead to obvious rewards on earth. Be honest about this with your kids. Admit that obeying God can lead to being laughed at, making less money, being misunderstood—even being killed. Balance this with a look at the rewards heaven offers.

Affirm your children's choices to obey God in the small things—when they choose to forgive a bully instead of getting revenge, when they visit a sick friend, when they turn down the chance to watch a forbidden movie. As they learn to surrender to God in the "minor" matters of daily life, they'll find it easier to surrender to Him in the bigger things.

Some children (and adults) fear that giving God control of their lives will lead to misery. For example, asking God to teach them patience will result in having to endure an itchy rash or a loud-mouthed classmate. Or surrendering to His plan will mean having to go to a country that features rainy weather, slimy food, and a language no one can learn. Assure your children that God is loving and kind. If they need to learn patience, they can trust God to teach them in the best possible way. If God wants to send them somewhere, He'll prepare them. God's goal isn't to ask them to do what they hate the most. He has an awesome plan for them.

GOD WANTS YOU TO CHOOSE HIS WAY BECAUSE YOU LOVE HIM AND WANT TO BE LIKE JESUS.

At this age, your children are making their own choices—including some you may not know about. How can you help them make the right ones?

Walk them through the decision-making process, using a real-life

MAKING TOUGH DECISIONS

What does the Bible have to say about making decisions? If your kids are facing tough choices, talk to them about these principles:

Don't rush to a decision but consider all the facts. "He who answers before listening—that is his folly and his shame" (Proverbs 18:13).

Ask the opinion of those you respect (such as your parents or other mature Christians). "Listen to advice and accept instruction, and in the end you will be wise" (Proverbs 19:20).

Ask God to give you wisdom. "If any of you lacks wisdom, he should ask God, who gives generously to all without finding fault, and it will be given to him" (James 1:5).

Read the Bible consistently and grow in your knowledge of God's ways. "Your word is a lamp to my feet and a light for my path" (Psalm 119:105).

---

choice they face. Help them weigh the pros and cons, see what God says about it, then choose the wisest course. Just as importantly, tell them why we need to choose right over wrong—out of love for God and a desire to be like Jesus: "And we know that in all things God works for the good of those who love him, who have been called according to his purpose" (Romans 8:28). No mere list of dos and don'ts will provide the motivation for your children to obey God over the long run. As you help them develop a closer relationship with God, that love and desire will grow as well: "Train a child in the way he should go, and when he is old he will not turn from it" (Proverbs 22:6).

Tempting as it might be to make all your children's decisions for them, it won't prepare them for the future. They need to learn how to tell right from wrong for themselves and how to make godly choices. You can begin this process by giving them "safe" arenas in which to choose. For example, let them decide whether to go to a particular church activity; then discuss their choice. Let them decide whether to study for a test; then discuss the results. To help you determine which choices are "safe" for them to make, take their maturity level and track record into account. Let them know that as they earn your trust, you'll trust them with more and more choices.

Discuss *ahead of time* the decisions children may face and how they'll handle them. For example, when your children are going over

to a friend's house to watch a video, help them decide in advance what kind of movie they'll watch or what they'll do if their friend wants to view something inappropriate. If they enjoy acting, do role-plays in which they act out various scenarios with different results.

When children have made a wrong choice, discuss what happened. Ask, "What other choices could you have made in this situation? How might you have done better?" Ask them to list the reasons for the decision they made. Then ask them to list reasons for a better choice they could have made, so that they can apply those reasons to other situations.

GOD WANTS YOU TO LEARN TO SEEK AND FOLLOW HIS SPIRIT'S LEADING.

To whom are your children listening? They probably hear plenty of advice from you, from peers, from teachers, from screens and CD players. But do they hear God's voice?

It's usually a still, small voice rather than an audible one. It takes practice to hear, a willingness to obey, and a turning away from distractions. But God's Spirit wants to guide your children into truth and remind them of Jesus' teaching: "But the Counselor, the Holy Spirit, whom the Father will send in my name, will teach you all things and will remind you of everything I have said to you" (John 14:26). You can help your children become more sensitive to God's leading as you teach them to listen for His influence on their thoughts as they pray, read the Bible, and hear the counsel of other Christians.

Have you ever felt God was telling you something through an event, something you read, a sermon you heard, or the words of a friend? If so, tell your children the story. What did you do about the "message"? What was the result?

Encourage your children to start the day by asking God to guide them. If they expect to face specific problems that day, it's a good idea to ask for specific direction. God may not hand them solutions right away, but they can trust Him to give them wisdom when the time comes: "It is because of him that you are in Christ Jesus, who has become for us wisdom from God—that is, our righteousness, holiness and redemption" (1 Corinthians 1:30).

To help children understand what it means to "hear God's voice," explain that God can communicate with us in any way He likes. Since His Spirit lives in those who belong to Him, He may sometimes help us to know things in our hearts without our having to hear them through our ears. Since our own thoughts and feelings may confuse us, it can be helpful to talk with a more experienced Christian before acting on the things we believe God has "told" us. One guideline to remember: God doesn't tell people things that disagree with what He's already said in the Bible. If we think God is telling us something, we should compare it with His Word to make sure there's no contradiction.

YOU NEED TO LEARN HOW TO RESIST SATAN AND TEMPTATION.

Your children need to know that they have an enemy: the devil, or Satan. It isn't necessary to talk about Satan and his demons a lot, but your children need the basic facts: "Above all, love each other deeply, because love covers over a multitude of sins" (1 Peter 4:8). The key fact is that when Jesus died and rose again, He defeated Satan. Still, when people do things Satan's way by disobeying God, they give the devil a foothold in their lives and let him accomplish some of his goals through them: " 'In your anger do not sin': Do not let the sun go down while you are still angry, and do not give the devil a foothold" (Ephesians 4:26-27).

When your children resist Satan by doing things God's way—making right decisions, asking for forgiveness when they sin—it's a victory for the winning side: "Submit yourselves, then, to God. Resist the devil, and he will flee from you" (James 4:7).

Tell your children that when they face temptation it's a good idea to turn to the Bible. When He was tempted, Jesus dealt with the devil's attacks by quoting Scripture. Your children can do what Jesus did—counter the devil's lies with verses they know (or can find) in the Bible, and choose God's way. Encourage them to pray when they're tempted, too—even if they're in the middle of making a mistake. When they ask for help, God will answer.

Reassure your children that even when they've blown it and given Satan a foothold, they can go to God for strength and forgiveness. You can model God's unconditional love by maintaining an open-door policy for your children when they've done wrong. Let them know that you're available for help and forgiveness, not just punishment.

Avoid giving your children the impression that the devil is scary. He's a master deceiver, a master liar. Seeking the truth and following God makes him powerless in our lives. Rather than railing against him (see Jude 9), however, let God judge him. Satan's fate is sealed. He's just trying to cause as much damage as he can before he's thrown into the lake of fire forever.

YOU NEED TO GET INVOLVED IN CHURCH AND FIND YOUR PLACE IN THE BODY OF CHRIST.

Your children aren't just the church of tomorrow. They're the church of today! You can help them see your church as *their* church and find a place to be involved. Kids don't have to wait until they grow up to be supportive of pastors and other leaders, or to give time, money, and energy to God's work.

Finding friends at church is a key to feeling part of it all. As your children get to know others at church, they'll feel an increasing sense of belonging and a desire to be there: "And let us consider how we may spur one another on toward love and good deeds. Let us not give up meeting together, as some are in the habit of doing, but let us encourage one another—and all the more as you see the Day approaching" (Hebrews 10:24-25).

> Your children aren't just the church of tomorrow. They're the church of today!

If you can find places for your children to help at church—places that fit their abilities and interests—they'll blossom. If they're outgoing, they might become greeters or join those who visit new families. Are they musical? Perhaps they can play or sing at meetings or join a youth choir. Do they like cooking? Let them help in the church kitchen or make goodies for a bake sale. Kids who like computers might help in the church office; budding artists could paint a mural in a Sunday school room; actors could put on skits or use puppets in children's church. If your children are starting to baby-sit or just like playing with younger kids, they might assist in the church nursery or with vacation Bible school.

How can you help your children find friends at church? If your kids are having trouble fitting in, talk with their Sunday school teacher or the person in charge of children's ministry at your church. Ask whether there are opportunities in the church's program for kids to get to know each other, perhaps in a club program, summer camp, or service project. Meet parents in your church whose children are in your kids' age range; invite these families over for dinner or another activity.

Are you enthused about church? Do you have a sense of belonging? Chances are that your children can tell whether church is a labor of love for you—or just labor. Expecting them to get fired up about something that leaves you cold is unrealistic. If that's the case with you, take the same steps for yourself that you'd take with your children. Find a spot to serve that taps into your gifts and passions. Join a small group that contains potential friends for you. As you gain a sense of belonging, your children will be more likely to think the same is possible for them: "They devoted themselves to the apostles' teaching and to the fellowship, to the breaking of bread and to prayer. . . . All the believers were together and had everything in common. . . . Every day they continued to meet together in the temple courts. They broke bread in their homes and ate together with glad and sincere hearts" (Acts 2:42, 44, 46).

ON THE BRINK OF THE TEEN YEARS
Check out this chart one more time to be amazed at what your 10-to-12-year-old children have been able to learn about God and their faith. Twelve years of consistent spiritual training is an awesome gift for launching your children into their teen years.

Ages 10–12

KNOWING		LOVING	LIVING	
A. Who God Is	B. What God Has Done	C. You Can Have a Relationship with God	D. You Can Be All God Wants You to Be	E. You Can Do All God Wants You to Do
1. Not everyone believes the truth about God, but there are ways you can respond to their objections. (Handling contrary opinions about God: basic apologetics; other religions)	2. God wants you to explore the One Big Story. 3. God put the Bible together in a fascinating way. 4. You need to learn how to study the Bible. 5. God lets His people serve Him and express their worship of Him in different ways. 6. God gave us an accurate record of His Son, Jesus. 7. God wants you to tell others about what Jesus has done. 8. Jesus will return as Judge and there will be a new heaven and a new earth.	9. You can pray on your own. 10. You can read the Bible on your own. 11. You can learn to worship God and Jesus on your own or in a group.	12. God wants you to choose to grow, learn, and seek His wisdom. 13. God's grace: You don't have to do it on your own. God is working in you by His Holy Spirit. 14. God wants you to find and follow His will for your life.	15. God wants you to choose to commit your entire life and everything you have to Him. 16. God wants you to choose His way because you love Him and want to be like Jesus. 17. God wants you to learn to seek and follow His Spirit's leading. 18. You need to learn how to resist Satan and temptation. 19. You need to get involved in church and find your place in the body of Christ.

CHAPTER 17

- - - - - - - - -

Great Expectations

How firm a foundation you have laid for your children's faith through your commitment to passing on the truths of God's Word through all the stages of their childhood! Here's a word of encouragement as they enter their teen years.

THE TEEN YEARS

At the end of the 10–12 stage, you need to be letting your children progressively take more responsibility for their own spiritual growth. The teen years they are heading into are an entirely different phase of life, and your role as a parent needs to change to match it. Your role moves toward becoming more like a coach, as opposed to an instructor and trainer. You now need to walk alongside your children and assist in their growth and discovery.

Young teenagers are beginning to have their own ideas of what they want and how to do things. They are in the process of formulating their identity: who they are in relation to you, their friends, and the world around them. They want to walk on their own two feet and be independent. Teens have strong opinions and are often confident that they can do quite well on their own, thank you very much. They are eagerly seeking signs that you approve of their growing independence as you give them more responsibility for making decisions and following through on them. For all these reasons, when your children hit their teen years, it is important to walk with them, coaching and guiding them, rather than always telling them what to do and how to do it.

The strong foundation that you have laid in their lives through spiritually training them in the early years will protect them and help them make the right decisions. The understanding of God, His ways, and His love will keep them following and seeking God. They are not entering a time when they know it all (in spite of what teens often think) and no longer need to grow and advance spiritually. They still need to have a personal relationship with God, read and study the Bible, be a part of a church, and live God's way. The difference is that they are now taking on responsibility for these things themselves with you encouraging them.

> When your children hit their teen years, it is important to walk with them, coaching and guiding them, rather than always telling them what to do and how to do it.

Be careful not to just let your teenagers go completely. Every coach checks up on the progress of his or her athletes or players. As your kids' coach, you need to watch their progress too. Here are four ways to do this.

1. Keep in touch with their progress by having regular conversations with them as a fellow learner. Tell them what you are learning, going through, and talking to God about, and then encourage them to include you in their spiritual lives.
2. Recruit them to assist you in teaching and helping with the spiritual growth of their younger siblings.
3. Encourage them to get involved in assisting with Sunday school classes at your church.
4. Pray for them every day.

Chapter 17

THE WAY OF LIFE

The life in Christ that each of your children has begun is an eternal life.
Their earthly, physical bodies will probably die someday,
but their new life in Christ will continue from now until
forever! Commit yourself to pray for your children—as
they enter their teen years and all throughout their adult
lives—that their early commitment to knowing who
God is and what He has done, to loving Him in an ever-
deepening relationship, and to living out their faith in
loving, joyful obedience will turn into a lifelong satisfying journey. Pray that God will show them "the way of life," granting
them the joy of His presence and the pleasures of living with God forever (Psalm 16:11).

> The life in Christ that each of your children has begun is an eternal life.

Appendix

God's One Big Story

In the beginning there were no rocks, trees, animals, stars, or people, only God—the Father, Son, and Holy Spirit. Then God made everything. After He had made the world and everything in it, God made people, Adam and Eve. God wanted to be a Father to them and have a wonderful, loving relationship with them. He made a beautiful garden for them to live in called Eden. God gave them one rule: Don't eat from the Tree of the Knowledge of Good and Evil.

But Satan, an important angel who became God's enemy, disguised himself as a snake and lied to them. Adam and Eve disobeyed God and ate the fruit from the forbidden tree. That was sin. It changed everything. God sent them out of the garden. He still loved them, but sin separates people from Him. Adam and Eve had a choice to love and obey God, or not. They chose to disobey. They didn't know how awful separation from God would be. Because of Adam and Eve's sin, everyone born after them was born sinful and separated from God, too. This meant people could no longer be God's children as He wanted. But God had a plan to bring people back to Him so they *could* be His children. He just needed one perfect person.

Adam and Eve had children, who had children, and so on until the world was full of sinful people. God was very sad. He decided to destroy everyone. But God found one man, Noah, who loved Him. He told Noah to build a huge boat called an ark. God sent two of most kinds of animals and seven of other kinds into the ark, along with Noah and his family. Then it began to rain. Forty days and nights later, only the people and animals in the ark were alive. And God was still working on His plan.

Noah's children had children, and so on until one day God chose a man named Abraham and his wife Sarah to be part of His plan. He told them He would be their God and sent them to a land called Canaan, which He promised to give their children forever. Abraham and Sarah were old and couldn't have children, but God gave them a miracle, a son named Isaac. God promised that one of Isaac's descendants—the Messiah, or Savior—would bless the whole world.

Isaac's son Jacob, also called Israel, had 12 sons and one daughter. Jacob gave his favorite son, Joseph, a special coat. Joseph's brothers were jealous and sold Joseph as a slave into Egypt. But even as a slave Joseph loved and obeyed God. Years later God helped him explain a dream to Pharaoh, the king of Egypt. The dream said a huge famine was coming. Pharaoh told Joseph to get Egypt ready for the famine by storing lots of food. When Joseph's family came to get food, Joseph invited them to live in Egypt.

The Israelites, Jacob's descendants, came to Egypt and had children who had children and so on. Years later, there were so many of them that the new Pharaoh got worried. He made them slaves and told them that they couldn't keep any of their baby boys. One Israelite mother set her baby boy, Moses, in a basket and put him in the river to escape Pharaoh. Pharaoh's daughter found him, took him to the palace, and raised him.

When Moses was a man, he killed an Egyptian who was mistreating a slave. Moses ran away to the desert. Years later he saw a bush on fire but not burning up. God spoke to him from the bush. He said, "Go to Egypt. Tell Pharaoh to let My people go!" God sent 10 plagues to show He was stronger than Egypt's false gods. In the last plague the oldest child in every family was to die. But God told the Israelites to kill lambs and put the blood on the doorways of their homes so He would pass over their houses and their children would be safe. The lambs died in place of the oldest children. This was called the Passover. That night Pharaoh let God's people go.

The Israelites left in a huge exodus, or exit. God led them into the desert and gave Moses the Ten Commandments and the Law, which told the Israelites how to please God and have a good life. Then God led them to the land He'd promised Abraham long ago. God was working out His plan.

Many years later, the Israelites asked God for a king. Their first king, Saul, fought their enemies, the Philistines. One day Goliath, a giant Philistine, made fun of God. A young Israelite boy named David trusted God and fought Goliath with only a sling and some stones. He won! Later God made him the king of Israel. David loved God with his whole heart.

For all those years, God was teaching people what He was like, but no one was ever perfect or sinless. Then, years and years later, God gave Mary, David's descendant, His own Son, Jesus, as a baby. God chose Joseph, Mary's fiancé, to help her look after Him. Because the baby was God's Son, He was born without sin. God sent angels to tell people about Jesus' birth. They came to see this amazing event: God's Son born as a baby!

Jesus grew up in Nazareth. When He was about 30, He began the job God had given Him. He was baptized in the Jordan River, then God led Him into the desert. Satan tempted Jesus to do things his way instead of God's, just as Satan had done to Adam and Eve. But Jesus refused.

Jesus taught people about God and His kingdom. He showed that God loved people by healing the sick, feeding the hungry, and loving those whom others didn't. He taught people how to have a good relationship with God.

The religious leaders were afraid that the people would follow Jesus instead of them, so they decided to get rid of Jesus. Judas, one of Jesus' followers, offered to help them arrest Him. Judas led guards to arrest Jesus. Then Jesus was put on trial for saying He was God's Son. The punishment was death. Jesus was beaten and led out to be crucified. But He asked God to forgive the people because they didn't realize what they were doing. Then, even though He really was the Son of God and He'd done nothing wrong, He died. He was the new Passover Lamb. (Remember the first one?)

After Jesus died, His friends put His body in a tomb. On the third day the tomb was empty! Jesus appeared to many people, proving He was alive again. God had accepted His death as payment for everyone's sins! Just as the Israelites were saved from death when they painted the lambs' blood on their doors, those who trust that Jesus died for their sins are saved. That meant the separation begun with Adam and Eve could be ended. All people could be God's children once again! Jesus was the perfect Messiah, or Savior, that God had promised long ago.

Jesus went up to heaven, but He sent the Holy Spirit to help His followers tell the world about Him and live the way God wanted. The religious leaders tried to stop them, but nothing worked. One leader, Saul, searched out Jesus' followers to have them arrested and killed. One day Jesus appeared to Saul, and he became a Christian that day. He changed his name to Paul and traveled the world telling people about Jesus. He started churches and wrote letters to help Christians live as God wanted them to. He also explained the teachings of Jesus and the Bible.

John, another one of Jesus' followers, was sent to an island prison for following Jesus. Jesus gave him a message for the church. In this message Jesus promises to come back and take God's children to be with Him in a new heaven and earth. There will be love and happiness there. No more sadness or pain. You'll be with God as His children, just as He planned before the world began. What a party that will be!

About the General Editors

DR. JOHN TRENT is president and founder of the Center for Strong Families and StrongFamilies.com, a ministry that trains lay leaders to build and lead marriage and family programs in their home churches. John speaks at conferences across the country and has authored and coauthored more than a dozen award-winning and best-selling books.

His books have been translated into 11 different languages, and there are more than 2 million copies of these adult and children's books in print. John has also been a featured guest on radio and television programs, such as *Focus on the Family, The 700 Club,* and CNN's *Sonya Live.*

John and his wife, Cindy, have been married for more than 26 years and have two daughters.

KURT BRUNER has authored books with combined sales of more than 500,000 copies, including *Your Heritage* and the best-selling Family Night Tool Chest series. A 1990 graduate of Talbot School of Theology and former Group Vice President over Media with Focus on the Family, he directed the creation of books, films, magazines, and audio drama. Kurt is cofounder of the Heritage Builders Association—a network of parents and churches committed to passing on a strong spiritual heritage to the next generation. He and his wife of more than 20 years, Olivia, are the parents of four and authors of *Playstation Nation: Protect Your Child from Video Game Addiction.* The Bruners also head up VideoGameTrouble.org.

RICK OSBORNE is a best-selling author and speaker committed to helping parents with the moral and spiritual development of their children. He coauthored *Teaching Your Child How to Pray, Bedtime Bible, God's Great News for Children,* and *801 Questions Kids Ask about God.* His most recent books are *Parenting at the Speed of Life* and *What Mary and Joseph Knew about Parenting.* He has been a key contributor in the development of the Luke 2:52 series, including *The Boys' Bible, Bible Heroes and Bad Guys,* and *Bible Wars and Weapons.*

He has written and cowritten more than 46 books and has been part of the development of more than 100 other church and parenting tools, books, and programs, all dedicated to raising children God's way. Rick's "story of Jesus" presentation book, *The Most Important Story Ever Told,* has had more than 50 million copies distributed worldwide in 110 different languages.

FOCUS ON THE FAMILY®

Welcome to the family!

Whether you purchased this book, borrowed it, or received it as a gift, we're glad you're reading it. It's just one of the many helpful, encouraging, and biblically based resources produced by Focus on the Family for people in all stages of life.

Focus began in 1977 with the vision of one man, Dr. James Dobson, a licensed psychologist and author of numerous best-selling books on marriage, parenting, and family. Alarmed by the societal, political, and economic pressures that were threatening the existence of the American family, Dr. Dobson founded Focus on the Family with one employee and a once-a-week radio broadcast aired on 36 stations.

Now an international organization reaching millions of people daily, Focus on the Family is dedicated to preserving values and strengthening and encouraging families through the life-changing message of Jesus Christ.

Focus on the Family Magazines

These faith-building, character-developing publications address the interests, issues, concerns, and challenges faced by every member of your family from preschool through the senior years.

| Focus on the Family **Citizen®** U.S. news issues | Focus on the Family **Clubhouse Jr.™** Ages 4 to 8 | Focus on the Family **Clubhouse™** Ages 8 to 12 | **Breakaway®** Teen guys | **Brio®** Teen girls 12 to 16 | **Brio & Beyond®** Teen girls 16 to 19 | **Plugged In®** Reviews movies, music, TV |

FOR MORE INFORMATION

Online:
Log on to www.family.org
In Canada, log on to www.focusonthefamily.ca

 Phone:
Call toll free: (800) A-FAMILY (232-6459)
In Canada, call toll free: (800) 661-9800

BP06XFM